U.S. Nuclear We

COUNCIL *on*
FOREIGN
RELATIONS

Independent Task Force Report No. 62

William J. Perry and Brent Scowcroft,
Chairs
Charles D. Ferguson, *Project Director*

U.S. Nuclear Weapons Policy

The Council on Foreign Relations (CFR) is an independent, nonpartisan membership organization, think tank, and publisher dedicated to being a resource for its members, government officials, business executives, journalists, educators and students, civic and religious leaders, and other interested citizens in order to help them better understand the world and the foreign policy choices facing the United States and other countries. Founded in 1921, CFR carries out its mission by maintaining a diverse membership, with special programs to promote interest and develop expertise in the next generation of foreign policy leaders; convening meetings at its headquarters in New York and in Washington, DC, and other cities where senior government officials, members of Congress, global leaders, and prominent thinkers come together with CFR members to discuss and debate major international issues; supporting a Studies Program that fosters independent research, enabling CFR scholars to produce articles, reports, and books and hold roundtables that analyze foreign policy issues and make concrete policy recommendations; publishing *Foreign Affairs*, the preeminent journal on international affairs and U.S. foreign policy; sponsoring Independent Task Forces that produce reports with both findings and policy prescriptions on the most important foreign policy topics; and providing up-to-date information and analysis about world events and American foreign policy on its website, www.cfr.org.

The Council on Foreign Relations takes no institutional position on policy issues and has no affiliation with the U.S. government. All statements of fact and expressions of opinion contained in its publications are the sole responsibility of the author or authors.

The Council on Foreign Relations sponsors Independent Task Forces to assess issues of current and critical importance to U.S. foreign policy and provide policymakers with concrete judgments and recommendations. Diverse in backgrounds and perspectives, Task Force members aim to reach a meaningful consensus on policy through private and nonpartisan deliberations. Once launched, Task Forces are independent of CFR and solely responsible for the content of their reports. Task Force members are asked to join a consensus signifying that they endorse "the general policy thrust and judgments reached by the group, though not necessarily every finding and recommendation." Each Task Force member also has the option of putting forward additional or dissenting views. Members' affiliations are listed for identification purposes only and do not imply institutional endorsement. Task Force observers participate in discussions, but are not asked to join the consensus.

For further information about CFR or this Task Force, please write to the Council on Foreign Relations, Communications, 58 East 68th Street, New York, NY 10065, or call Communications at 212.434.9400. Visit CFR's website at www.cfr.org.

This report is printed on paper certified by SmartWood to the standards of the Forest Stewardship Council, which promotes environmentally responsible, socially beneficial, and economically viable management of the world's forests.

Mixed Sources

Product group from well-managed forests, controlled sources and recycled wood or fiber

www.fsc.org Cert no. SW-COC-001530
© 1996 Forest Stewardship Council

FSC

Task Force Members

Task Force members are asked to join a consensus signifying that they endorse "the general policy thrust and judgments reached by the group, though not necessarily every finding and recommendation." They participate in the Task Force in their individual, not institutional, capacities.

Spencer P. Boyer

Linton F. Brooks

Ashton B. Carter*

John Deutch†

Charles D. Ferguson

Michèle A. Flournoy*

John A. Gordon

Lisa E. Gordon-Hagerty

Eugene E. Habiger

J. Bryan Hehir

Laura S.H. Holgate†

Frederick J. Iseman

Arnold Kanter

Ronald F. Lehman II†

Jack F. Matlock Jr.

Franklin C. Miller

George R. Perkovich†

William J. Perry

Mitchell B. Reiss

Lynn Rusten

Scott D. Sagan†

Brent Scowcroft

Benn Tannenbaum†

*Carter and Flournoy participated in the Task Force under their affiliations with Harvard University and the Center for a New American Security, respectively. As current administration officials, they have not been asked to join the Task Force consensus.

†The individual has endorsed the report and submitted an additional or dissenting view.

_− 62_

Contents

Foreword

On his first trip to Europe as president, Barack Obama stood in Prague and reaffirmed the U.S. commitment to a world free of nuclear weapons: "As the only nuclear power to have used a nuclear weapon, the United States has a moral responsibility to act. We cannot succeed in this endeavor alone, but we can lead it, we can start it." President Obama also outlined a series of near-term steps to support this long-term goal, including the negotiation of a new nuclear arms reduction treaty with Russia and measures to strengthen the international nuclear nonproliferation regime.

The question of whether and how to move toward the elimination of nuclear weapons has emerged as a central foreign policy issue. But that vision remains just a vision. President Obama himself has acknowledged that "this goal will not be reached quickly—perhaps not in my lifetime." Meanwhile, there are critical questions to be addressed about nuclear weapons and policy.

The Council on Foreign Relations convened an Independent Task Force to assess these questions of nuclear weapons and make recommendations concerning U.S. forces and policies. The report notes that in the near term nuclear weapons will remain a fundamental element of U.S. national security. For this reason it emphasizes the importance of maintaining a safe, secure, and reliable deterrent nuclear force and makes recommendations on this front. The report also offers measures to advance important goals such as preventing nuclear terrorism and bolstering the nuclear nonproliferation regime.

The report notes that because of the impending Nonproliferation Treaty Review and the U.S. government's nuclear posture review, the Obama administration has a unique opportunity to examine existing policies and agreements and take new steps in a number of areas. Although Task Force members disagreed on the practicality and desirability of eventual nuclear abolition, the report supports deeper reductions in U.S. and Russian arsenals. The Task Force also calls for a revived strategic dialogue between the United States and Russia, as well as renewed military-to-military discussions with China to encourage transparency on both sides on strategic and nuclear security issues. In addition, it favors ratification of the Comprehensive Test Ban Treaty and recommends a halt to the production of fissile material for weapons. Finally, the report calls on the United States to reaffirm security assurances to its allies and puts forth a set of best security practices for all states that have nuclear weapons and weapons-usable fissile material.

On behalf of the Council on Foreign Relations, I wish to thank Task Force chairs and distinguished public servants William J. Perry and Brent Scowcroft, whose knowledge, insight, and standing were integral to leading this effort. CFR is also indebted to the individual Task Force members, who each contributed his or her significant experience and expertise to the report. My thanks go as well to Anya Schmemann, director of CFR's Task Force program, who guided this project from start to finish. I also thank Charles D. Ferguson, CFR's Philip D. Reed senior fellow for science and technology, for ably and patiently directing the project and writing the report. The hard work of all those involved has produced an important study that outlines a responsible agenda for U.S. nuclear policy in an era that poses unprecedented nuclear threats but also historic opportunities.

Richard N. Haass
President
Council on Foreign Relations
April 2009

Chairs' Preface

Every day during the Cold War, the world faced the possibility of a nuclear exchange that could have resulted in the end of civilization. With those times past, the danger of a nuclear holocaust might seem remote. But the end of the Cold War did not also bring about the end of history. History is being written every day, in the streets of Baghdad, in the nuclear test ranges of North Korea, in the nuclear labs of Iran, in the council chambers of the Kremlin, and in the Great Hall of the People in Beijing.

So, although the world no longer lives under the threat of a nuclear holocaust, these remain dangerous times. American service personnel are still being killed in Iraq. The Taliban is resurging in Afghanistan and Pakistan. North Korea has tested a nuclear bomb, and Iran is not far behind. Russia's relations with the United States have become strained, with the tension reaching dangerous levels during the crisis in Georgia in 2008.

The first decade after the Cold War ended was one of euphoria, but that has faded. All the daunting security challenges that have manifested themselves over the last decade now confront the new president. Three security challenges in particular will require priority action by the Obama administration:

- stopping and reversing the ongoing proliferation of nuclear weapons,
- reducing the risk of terrorists conducting nuclear attacks, and
- reducing the risk of the United States and Russia drifting into a hostile relationship with some of the dangers of the Cold War.

Despite nearly universal opposition, North Korea has developed a small nuclear arsenal, and Iran appears to be following in its footsteps. Other states, particularly in the Middle East, are starting nuclear power programs modeled after that of Iran. The proliferation of nuclear weapons and fissile materials is thus dangerously close to a tipping point. Beyond this danger, there are still tens of thousands of nuclear weapons in the world. If just one of these thousands of weapons fell into the hands of terrorists, it could be detonated with catastrophic results. So, although the old danger of a massive nuclear exchange between great powers has declined, a new risk looms of a few nuclear detonations being set off by a terrorist group or a nuclear-capable rogue state, or of a nuclear power making a tragic mistake. The threat of nuclear terrorism is already serious, and, as more nations acquire nuclear weapons or the fissile material needed for nuclear weapons, it will increase.

Of course, the detonation of a relatively primitive nuclear bomb in one American city would not be equivalent to the type of nuclear exchange that was feared during the Cold War. Nonetheless, the results would be catastrophic, with the devastation extending well beyond the staggering fatalities. The direct economic losses would amount to many hundreds of billions of dollars, but the indirect economic impact would be even greater. The social and political effects are incalculable, especially if the detonation were in Washington, DC, and disabled a significant part of the U.S. government. The terror and disruption would be beyond imagination.

High priority should be accorded to policies that serve to prevent such a catastrophe, specifically programs that reduce and protect existing nuclear arsenals and that keep new arsenals from being created. All such preventive programs, by their nature, have international dimensions. Their success depends on the United States being able to work cooperatively with other countries, most notably Russia. That such international cooperation can be successful is illustrated by the Nunn-Lugar Cooperative Threat Reduction Program in the 1990s. U.S.-Russian efforts on that program led to thousands of nuclear weapons and their launchers being dismantled and thus made the world safer. But unless U.S.-Russia relations improve, it is difficult to imagine those two governments cooperating on future programs that require such a high level of mutual trust.

The threat of a nuclear conflict is also not totally removed. Russia retains the capability to pose an existential threat to the United States. However, since the end of the Cold War, Russia has neither shown nor threatened such intent against the United States. Indeed, for much of this period the United States and Russia cooperated closely on reducing nuclear arsenals and curbing nuclear proliferation. The most recent chill in U.S.-Russia relations has been caused in part by U.S. efforts to make Ukraine and Georgia members of the North Atlantic Treaty Organization (NATO) and to deploy elements of a missile defense system in Poland and the Czech Republic. Additionally, Russia has begun to rebuild its nuclear forces. These developments are not remotely equivalent to the hostility during the Cold War, but ignoring such problems could lead to the resurfacing of certain Cold War–like tensions.

The Obama administration, understanding the importance of this issue, has begun a major effort to restart a strategic dialogue with Russia. In a speech in Munich just a few weeks after the inauguration, Vice President Joseph Biden proposed to "press the reset button" on U.S.-Russia relations. President Obama and Russian president Dmitry Medvedev met in April and announced their intent to negotiate a new arms control treaty and make deeper reductions in their nuclear arsenals. We strongly support this dialogue, which includes their common interest in nuclear nonproliferation, but recognize that success is far from assured. The United States and Russia have been far apart on other issues, most notably NATO expansion, missile defense deployment in eastern Europe, and the relative importance of so-called "tactical" nuclear weapons. Yet, understanding what is at stake, it is encouraging to see both sides moving to make a fresh start.

Besides working to reduce American and Russian arsenals, the Obama administration should do everything it reasonably can to keep new arsenals from being created. North Korea has already built a small nuclear arsenal and shows no signs of being willing to negotiate it away, and Iran could prove to be an even more dangerous proliferator. The European Union and Russia have had no significant success in restraining Iran's nuclear program. The Bush administration was reluctant to get involved in discussions with Iran without preconditions. It seems clear that any chance of success with North Korea and Iran will require aggressive diplomacy that fully involves the Obama administration in close cooperation with other relevant international actors. This process has already begun, with the recent London talks of the permanent five members of the UN Security Council plus Germany, which culminated in a decision to invite Iran to participate in future discussions.

Beyond North Korea and Iran, dozens of other nations could become nuclear powers but have voluntarily refrained from doing so under the Nuclear Nonproliferation Treaty (NPT). To sustain these states' continuing support for the NPT, the United States and the other four nuclear weapon states need to demonstrate that they are each carrying out their responsibilities under the NPT—that is, moving seriously toward eliminating their nuclear weapons. The Obama administration has stated that it intends to work for the ultimate global elimination of nuclear weapons, but that until that goal is achieved it will maintain a safe, secure, and reliable deterrent. It will at a minimum be many years before the goal of zero nuclear weapons can be realized, and thus the United States should set a goal of reaching what some have called a base camp or vantage point. The steps leading to this shorter-term goal should reduce nuclear dangers from their present level. When that goal is reached, it will be possible to reevaluate whether geopolitical conditions permit moving closer to the elimination of nuclear weapons. That decision need not be made now and, indeed, it is not possible now to envision the geopolitical conditions that would permit moving toward the final goal. The objective of ensuring that a nuclear weapon is never used is central to creating the political conditions that would allow the world to take practical, near-term actions to make us far safer than we are at this moment.

Of the various actions recommended in this report, we would like, as chairs, to call special attention to the following actions designed to reduce global nuclear dangers:

- State clearly that it is a U.S. goal to prevent nuclear weapons from ever being used, by either a state or a nonstate actor, and that the sole purpose of U.S. nuclear weapons is providing deterrence for the United States and its allies.
- Reaffirm support for the agreed positive and negative security assurances that the United States has made to nonnuclear NPT states.
- Continue to reduce reliance on nuclear weapons and do so in a transparent manner; take the international lead in reducing the salience of nuclear weapons in security policy.
- Seek further reductions and greater stability in nuclear forces; these reductions would initially need to be made in a bilateral agreement with Russia. (Other aspects of the agreement—verification procedures, downloading and attribution rules, and stability features—will probably be more important than the actual numbers.)

- Seek to ratify the Comprehensive Test Ban Treaty (CTBT), first assembling an expert group to analyze the policy and technical issues related to the CTBT and then presenting the treaty for Senate ratification; if successful in ratifying the treaty, work with other holdout nations to do the same.
- Restart discussions on a Fissile Material Cutoff Treaty (FMCT), including provisions for verification.
- Strengthen the International Atomic Energy Agency's vital role of containing proliferation; this would include seeking universal adoption of the Additional Protocol and also Security Council review when nations withdraw from the NPT.

While taking these actions to reduce the danger of nuclear weapons, the United States will also be undertaking programs designed to maintain its nuclear deterrent. The Obama administration will have the responsibility of preparing later this year a new Strategic Posture Review that describes how maintaining the deterrent will be accomplished. The statement should be based on the following two policies: affirming that, for the foreseeable future, the United States will continue to maintain nuclear forces capable of providing credible deterrence for itself and its allies; and backing up this deterrent and extended deterrence policy with nuclear forces that are safe, secure, and reliable, and exist in adequate quantities to perform their deterrent role.

To carry out these policies, the United States will have to make decisions on how to most effectively maintain its nuclear weapons programs. A high priority is sustaining the effectiveness of the Stockpile Stewardship Program and the Life Extension Program, which provide the technical basis for maintaining the safety, security, and reliability of U.S. nuclear forces into the future. The nuclear weapons labs have achieved remarkable success in the Stockpile Stewardship Program since it was created in 1997, a result attributable to the skill of their staff, the leadership of their directors, and the necessary funding support. Sustaining this level of success, however, is endangered by ongoing reductions in funding for lab personnel. The administration should restore the funding of these programs to the levels of a few years ago.

The Life Extension Program has also been successful, but faces the same problems in personnel funding. Additionally, it will become increasingly difficult to sustain the reliability of weapons designed and tested several decades ago. The labs will need to be given authority either to undertake redesigns (with the same military mission and without testing) or to undertake an enhanced Life Extension Program that would include mining components from unused weapons. Decisions on which approach to take should be made on a case-by-case basis, weighing heavily the recommendations from the nuclear weapons lab responsible for the particular weapon being considered.

Finally, the aging nuclear physical infrastructure should be modernized to a much smaller yet sustainable pilot production capability. This modernization, though important, can be phased in over time and should not be funded by a reduction in force of lab personnel, as is now proposed.

The dangers of nuclear proliferation and nuclear terrorism are real and imminent, and any serious effort to reduce them will require the leadership of the United States. The risk of a new Cold War–like hostility developing between the United States and Russia is also real, and efforts to reduce it will require opening a positive strategic dialogue with Russia, at the same time hedging against the possibility that such a dialogue may not be successful. In short, the nuclear policy of the United States should be to lead when possible and hedge when necessary.

William J. Perry
Brent Scowcroft
Task Force Chairs

Acknowledgments

The debate over U.S. nuclear weapons policy is persistent and complex. Reaching a consensus and creating a set of meaningful findings and recommendations to inform this debate proved to be a challenging task for the Independent Task Force on U.S. Nuclear Weapons Policy. I am deeply indebted, therefore, to the insight and expertise of its two chairs, distinguished public servants and "wise men" William J. Perry and Brent Scowcroft. They guided the group toward accord on a broad range of issues. It has been a pleasure and an honor to work with them.

In addition to our chairs, the dedicated members and observers of this Task Force must be commended for their knowledge, pragmatism, and patience throughout this process. Special thanks are owed to those members who went the extra mile by participating in additional study group meetings on Russia and nonproliferation.

Along the way, many colleagues outside of the Task Force graciously offered their opinions on the content of the report and their advice on the process by which to reach consensus. I am especially appreciative of the help provided by Richard Butler, Deepti Choubey, Jonathan Granoff, Robert T. Grey Jr., Morton H. Halperin, Daryl Kimball, Jeffrey G. Lewis, Dunbar Lockwood, Joseph F. Pilat, Arian L. Pregenzer, and Andrew Robb.

A number of people at the Council on Foreign Relations helped bring this effort to fruition. In the early stages of the project, Lisa Obrentz and Lindsay Workman worked diligently to identify potential members and to conduct research to define the scope of the Task Force. Michelle M. Smith then stepped in to organize meetings, communicate with members, edit and revise the report, and coordinate its distribution. From beginning to end, Anya Schmemann and Swetha Sridharan skillfully guided the Task Force, editing multiple drafts of the report, providing guidance on the Task Force process, and coordinating with the rest of the organization. Once completed, Patricia Dorff and Lia

C. Norton readied the report for publication. Irina A. Faskianos and her team organized review sessions with CFR members in Atlanta, Boston, Chicago, and Pittsburgh. Nancy D. Bodurtha and Kay King led the Meetings departments in organizing preview and release events for CFR members in New York and Washington, DC. CFR's Communications, Corporate, External Affairs, and Outreach teams worked hard to get the report into the right hands, even in the midst of the transition to a new administration.

I am particularly grateful to CFR President Richard N. Haass for giving me the opportunity to direct this important effort. The Independent Task Force on U.S. Nuclear Weapons Policy was made possible in part by generous grants from the Carnegie Corporation of New York and the Ploughshares Fund. We also thank David M. Rubenstein for his support of the Task Force program and the Robina Foundation for its support of CFR's work on nuclear energy and nuclear nonproliferation through the International Institutions and Global Governance program.

I stipulate here that the statements made and views expressed within this document are solely the responsibility of the Task Force members. Once again, my thanks go to all who assisted in this effort. It is my hope that the Task Force report can serve as a resource in the transformation of U.S. nuclear weapons policy.

Charles D. Ferguson
Project Director

Acronyms

ABM	Anti-Ballistic Missile
CPPNM	Convention on Physical Protection of Nuclear Material
CTBT	Comprehensive Test Ban Treaty
CTR	Cooperative Threat Reduction Program [Nunn-Lugar]
FMCT	Fissile Material Cutoff Treaty
GTRI	Global Threat Reduction Initiative
HEU	highly enriched uranium
IAEA	International Atomic Energy Agency
ICBM	intercontinental ballistic missile
INF	intermediate-range nuclear forces
LEU	low-enriched uranium
MIRV	multiple independently targetable reentry vehicle
NATO	North Atlantic Treaty Organization
NNSA	National Nuclear Security Administration
NPT	Treaty on the Nonproliferation of Nuclear Weapons
RNEP	robust nuclear earth penetrator
RRW	reliable replacement warhead
SLBM	submarine-launched ballistic missile
SORT	Strategic Offensive Reductions Treaty [Moscow]
SSBN	ballistic missile submarine
START	Strategic Arms Reduction Treaty
STRATCOM	U.S. Strategic Command

WINS	World Institute for Nuclear Security
WMD	weapons of mass destruction
WSSX	Warhead Safety and Security Exchange

A Note on Definitions

A number of terms are used to describe the U.S. nuclear weapons stockpile. This report uses the following terms, which are consistent with those used by the government.

- *Operationally deployed strategic weapons/warheads* are warheads installed on intercontinental ballistic missiles (ICBMs) and submarine-launched ballistic missiles (SLBMs), plus bombs and cruise missile warheads at bomber bases. The officially approved 2012 force level of 1,700 to 2,200 warheads and the limits of the Strategic Offensive Reductions Treaty (SORT), or the Moscow Treaty, refer to this number.
- *Deployed nonstrategic warheads* are the small number of tactical bombs retained in Europe. The exact number has not been made public.
- *Reserve warheads* are the combination of logistic spares (replacements for warheads in maintenance) and responsive capability (warheads available to replace unreliable warheads or to augment the deployed force in response to geopolitical changes). The exact number has not been made public.
- *Stockpile* is the total number of warheads authorized by the president to be in the custody of the Department of Defense and is the sum of the three listed categories. When the George W. Bush administration used formulations such as "smallest stockpile since the Eisenhower administration," it was referring to this number.[1]

In addition, there are two other categories *not* considered part of the stockpile.

- *Retired warheads* are nonfunctional warheads in the custody of the Department of Energy awaiting disassembly. The exact number has not been made public.
- *Dismantled warheads or components* are warheads that have been reduced to their component parts. Plutonium pits from dismantled warheads are stored at the Pantex plant in Amarillo, Texas, and uranium components are stored at the Y-12 plant near Oak Ridge, Tennessee.

Task Force Report

Executive Summary

For more than sixty years, the United States and the world have benefited immeasurably from a de facto taboo on the use of nuclear weapons. Today, however, this period of nonuse may come to an end, given the rise of a new type of terrorist who seeks to acquire and would not hesitate to detonate nuclear weapons. Moreover, the emergence of more states with nuclear weapons capabilities has raised the likelihood of the use or loss of control of nuclear weapons or the materials used to make them. The imperative before the Obama administration, therefore, is to use all available tools to prevent the use and further acquisition of nuclear weapons. This Task Force report identifies how to leverage U.S. nuclear weapons posture and policy to achieve that objective. It focuses on near-term steps, primarily over the next four years.

President Barack Obama has pledged to "set a goal of a world without nuclear weapons, and pursue it,"[2] but he has also said that until that goal is reached, he will maintain a "safe, secure, and effective arsenal to deter any adversary."[3] The geopolitical conditions that would permit the global elimination of nuclear weapons do not currently exist, but this Task Force has identified many steps that are available in the near term that can greatly reduce the danger of nuclear proliferation and nuclear use. The Task Force is divided on the practicality or even desirability of a world without nuclear weapons, but those members who support it commend the president's pledge to work for global elimination and believe that his pledge will facilitate achieving those steps. Further, all members of the Task Force agree on the necessity of working toward reducing these dangers.

The Task Force underscores that renewed U.S. leadership to shape global nuclear weapons policy and posture is critical. Many competing interests demand President Obama's attention, but the impending expiration of the Strategic Arms Reduction Treaty (START) in December 2009, the upcoming congressionally mandated nuclear posture review, and the preparation for the 2010 Nonproliferation Treaty Review Conference offer the new administration an opportunity to begin to review existing treaties, revive negotiations, strengthen the global nonproliferation system, and promote best nuclear security efforts. In addition, for the United States to have credibility in arguing that others must restrain their nuclear ambitions, it must reexamine the size and composition of its own arsenal. The Task Force emphasizes that the United States has a particular opportunity in the renewal of arms control talks with Russia and urges a revitalized strategic dialogue with Russian leaders. Further, the Task Force urges the United States and Russia, as the two states possessing more than 90 percent of the world's nuclear warheads, to lead efforts in establishing best nuclear security practices worldwide.

The report underscores the need to strengthen nuclear risk reduction with the two major nuclear-armed states of Russia and China. The U.S. and Russian presidents recently pledged to reduce their nuclear arsenals. The Task Force supports efforts to renew legally binding arms control pacts with Russia by seeking follow-on agreements to START and the 2002 Strategic Offensive Reductions Treaty (SORT). The report also urges the United States and Russia to initiate a serious strategic dialogue, because it is only through such engagement that they can open up opportunities for deeper reductions in their arsenals and gain a better sense of the feasibility of moving toward multilateral nuclear arms control.

The United States and China, however, are not yet ready to form a formal nuclear arms control agreement because of the significant asymmetry between their two arsenals. Nonetheless, the report recommends that the two countries engage in a serious discussion of weapons in space. The United States, China, and Russia have all demonstrated their antisatellite weapons capabilities and have a strong interest in ensuring the security of their civilian and military satellites. The report proposes a ban on the testing of antisatellite weapons, which should include Russia and eventually be globally applicable.

The report's scope concentrates on U.S. nuclear posture, policy, and arms control; it does not directly focus on political and military strategies toward emergent nuclear weapons-capable states such as Iran and North Korea, though the proliferation challenges posed by these countries are discussed.[4]

One of this report's main themes relevant for nonproliferation is that with rights come responsibilities. In particular, all nonnuclear weapon states have the right to access and use peaceful nuclear energy, but that right is contingent on these states not seeking to acquire nuclear explosives and maintaining adequate safeguards on their nuclear programs to give other states confidence that these programs remain peaceful. The recognized nuclear weapon states under the 1970 Nonproliferation Treaty (NPT) already have mature nuclear power programs, and should consider placing their civilian nuclear programs under safeguards as an example to the nonnuclear weapon states. Similarly, the Task Force believes that these nations, including the United States, have the responsibility to reduce their nuclear weapons programs to the lowest possible level consistent with maintaining a credible deterrent, and work toward the goal of achieving multilateral nuclear arms reductions. All parties to the NPT—both nuclear and nonnuclear weapon states—share the obligation under Article VI to pursue nuclear as well as general and complete disarmament.

In line with the NPT's call for nuclear disarmament, the Task Force urges all states, both nuclear and nonnuclear, to accept their shared responsibility for reducing the risks of nuclear weapons acquisition and use. In addition, the Task Force recommends the development and implementation of best physical security practices in all states that have nuclear weapons and weapons-usable fissile material, including in their civilian programs, to reduce the risk of nuclear terrorism.

Another security pillar is for the United States to ensure that allies are protected against nuclear attack. Although the United States does not need nuclear weapons to compensate for conventional military weaknesses, other states are not in a similar position—they may consider acquiring nuclear weapons to deter attacks. The United States has the responsibility to assure allies through extended deterrence commitments. This assurance helps convince many of these allies to not acquire their own nuclear weapons, thereby improving the nonproliferation system. The Task Force supports having the Obama administration reaffirm these commitments.

A related pillar, necessary to maintain the credibility of the U.S. nuclear deterrent for as long as it is needed, is to ensure that the U.S. nuclear arsenal is safe, secure, and reliable. The U.S. nuclear weapons complex needs to be able to attract and retain highly competent scientists, engineers, and managers and have sufficient financial and technical resources to maintain the credibility of the deterrent. The Task Force supports a nuclear weapons security enterprise that stresses the equal importance of nonproliferation, prevention of nuclear terrorism, facilitation of verifiable nuclear arms reductions, and maintenance of a credible nuclear arsenal.

Along these lines, the Task Force recommends that the administration perform a detailed analysis, with an emphasis on political and military costs and benefits, of the proposals to build replacement warheads and transform the nuclear weapons complex. The Task Force offers the following guidelines to the administration as it makes an assessment on whether to build replacement warheads: no new nuclear testing, no new military capabilities, additional safety and security features, and substantial reductions in reserve warheads.

Similarly, the Task Force supports a transformation of the nuclear weapons complex, or complex transformation, that would ensure significant cost savings, a substantially reduced footprint for the overall complex, accelerated dismantlement of decommissioned warheads, and disposal—as much as is feasible—of excess highly enriched uranium (HEU) and plutonium from the weapons program into nonweapons-usable forms. In all of these activities, the Task Force believes that the United States has a strong interest in transparency about U.S. decisions on nuclear posture and the future of the weapons complex.

An additional pillar of a strengthened nuclear system is that every state with nuclear weapons or weapons-usable materials has the responsibility to implement best security practices. Fissile material that can directly be used in nuclear weapons should be kept as secure as intact weapons. There is a particular need for cooperative nuclear security work with India and Pakistan. The United States should frame such security activities as a sharing of lessons learned and not as an effort to impose a particular security method. The object here is to ensure that all nuclear-armed states continually reevaluate the security of their nuclear weapons and materials, including frequent intelligence community assessment of potential terrorist and nonstate actor threats.

The United States cannot form a more effective nuclear security system alone. It must work cooperatively with global partners. All states share the responsibility to ensure that nuclear weapons are never used again, to prevent the acquisition of additional nuclear weapons by other states, and to redouble efforts to secure and reduce existing nuclear weapons and weapons-usable materials. However, as President Obama said in Prague, "the United States has a moral responsibility to act. We cannot succeed in this endeavor alone, but we can lead it, we can start it."[5]

The Need for a New Policy Assessment

In recent years, the dangers associated with nuclear weapons and the complexities of addressing these dangers have steadily grown. The United States faces a daunting set of challenges, including the risk of nuclear terrorism, threats from emerging nuclear states such as Iran and North Korea, the illicit transfer of nuclear technologies through black markets, the potential for loss of control of nuclear weapons or weapons-usable materials, especially those from Pakistan, the increased importance of nuclear weapons in Russia's defense planning, and the uncertainty in China's strategic development. The Task Force believes that these challenges demand a reassessment of U.S. nuclear weapons policy to help guide the new administration, especially in preparing for the upcoming congressionally mandated nuclear posture review and 2010 NPT Review Conference.

Even one nuclear explosion, causing destruction anywhere, would have a catastrophic impact on U.S. and international security and profoundly change human history. More important than ever, therefore, is the fundamental objective of U.S. nuclear policy—to prevent the use of nuclear weapons by any state or nonstate actor and the spread of nuclear weapons capabilities to additional states or any nonstate actors. The Task Force strongly supports this objective as the primary mission of U.S. nuclear policy.

Recognizing that achieving this objective requires a careful balance among potentially competing efforts, this report assesses the following U.S. strategies:

- reviving a vigorous strategic dialogue with Russia and China;
- renewing legally binding arms control with Russia to achieve deeper nuclear arms reductions;
- preventing more states or any nonstate actors from acquiring nuclear weapons or nuclear weapons capabilities;

7

- limiting the spread of weapons-usable nuclear technologies;
- reaffirming security assurances to allies;
- securing and reducing the number of nuclear weapons and the amount of weapons-usable nuclear materials;
- determining how and when to bring other nuclear-armed states into the arms control process; and
- ensuring that as long as the United States maintains nuclear weapons, its arsenal is safe, secure, and reliable.

This report primarily addresses three principal challenges that confront the United States: first, the risks of dangerous misperceptions or miscalculations between the United States and Russia; second, the emergence of more nuclear weapons-capable states; and, third, nuclear terrorism. On the threat of nuclear terrorism, traditional deterrence would not work, because stateless terrorists have no national territory that the United States could threaten to target to deter them from using nuclear weapons, though it might be able to deter the state sponsors of these groups if there were any. Another challenging issue is the availability of nuclear weapons and materials manufactured by states to terrorist groups, either through deliberate action or negligent security. The likelihood of nuclear terrorists acquiring the capability to produce weapons-usable fissile material is extremely low. They would, instead, have to acquire this material from state stockpiles.

This observation leads logically to the conclusion that the likelihood of nuclear terrorism could be significantly reduced if nuclear weapons were verifiably abolished and weapons-usable fissile material was eliminated. However, all nuclear-armed countries still rely on nuclear weapons for deterrence, and several nonnuclear weapon states, such as Canada, Japan, Germany, and South Africa, possess weapons-usable fissile material for civilian applications. Further, there is no obvious way to verify elimination of either nuclear weapons or material. Thus, the United States and other governments need to find the proper balance between two important priorities—reducing nuclear weapons and weapons-usable fissile material while increasing the security of the remaining weapons and material to lessen the risk of nuclear terrorism, and maintaining the appropriate numbers and types of nuclear weapons for national security purposes.

OPPORTUNITIES FOR U.S. LEADERSHIP

To set the stage for the report's analysis of how U.S. nuclear weapons policy can substantially reduce nuclear dangers, it is important to stress a central issue underlying the primary objective and strategies. That is, political relationships fundamentally matter. The United States cannot make a more secure world alone. The start of a new administration presents a fresh opportunity to reenergize international dialogue and cooperation on best security practices that would reduce the risk of loss of control of nuclear weapons or materials. Strategic discussions with other nuclear-armed states would also provide the United States with the necessary insight and foresight to determine how best to shape U.S. nuclear policy.

Looming deadlines highlight the action required and the opportunities for the Obama administration to reenergize national and international efforts to further secure and reduce nuclear weapons and weapons-usable materials. Congress requires the administration to conduct an official nuclear posture review, which will likely take place through 2009 and perhaps into 2010. The expiration of START in December 2009 provides the administration with an opportunity to work with Russia to create a follow-on treaty that can lead to deeper cuts in the American and Russian nuclear arsenals. (The challenges implicit in this bilateral negotiation are explored in detail later in this report.)

In May 2010, the NPT Review Conference will take place. To prepare for it, the administration will have had just over a year to assemble a diplomatic team and form an effective strategy for sustaining the nonproliferation regime. This regime has suffered shocks in recent years because of North Korea's withdrawal from the treaty, subsequent production of weapons-grade plutonium, and detonation of a nuclear device, and Iran's noncompliance with its nuclear safeguards agreement. In addition to working toward further nuclear arms reductions with Russia and shoring up the nonproliferation regime, the Task Force points to the critical need for U.S. leadership on strategic dialogue with other nuclear-armed states and cooperative work with all states to strengthen nuclear security practices.

The Task Force recognizes the economic crisis and nonnuclear policy challenges facing the new administration. Nonetheless, as long as the new nuclear security and nonproliferation teams have clear presidential guidance and support, the task of reinforcing U.S. leadership in efforts to improve the nuclear nonproliferation regime and maintain a strong deterrent should be achievable. The United States, even faced with an economic crisis, should not shortchange protecting against a nuclear attack, however limited, that could cause damage of many trillions of dollars.

At the NPT Review Conference, the United States and other nuclear-armed states should be prepared to explain the reasons for their nuclear policies and postures. Thus, at the outset, this report examines post–Cold War changes in U.S. nuclear policy and posture, foreign perceptions of those changes, and the current and foreseeable purposes of U.S. nuclear weapons.

POST–COLD WAR CHANGES IN U.S. NUCLEAR WEAPONS POSTURE AND POLICY

Since the end of the Cold War, the United States has dismantled thousands of nuclear weapons. Although it has not published the exact number of dismantled warheads or the remaining number in the arsenal, unofficial estimates are that the U.S. arsenal contains about five thousand to six thousand warheads. This amount includes a few thousand in either deployed or readily deployable status, with the remainder in reserve. The United States committed to reducing the deployed total to between 1,700 and 2,200 warheads (the limits of SORT) by the end of 2012, and has reportedly already reached this level.[6] However, in addition to these, the United States has a large number of warheads in reserve that it could upload on existing missiles and a large backlog of warheads slated for dismantlement. As discussed in more detail later, the same facility that reassembles warheads, as part of the Life Extension Program, also disassembles or dismantles them. Thus, there is a trade-off between the rates of reassembly and dismantlement. But the fissile cores, known as plutonium pits, of the dismantled warheads have not yet been converted into nonweapons-usable forms. About fourteen thousand of these pits are stored at the Pantex plant in Amarillo, Texas, and are thus able to be reused. From the standpoint of U.S. leadership in nuclear terrorism risk reduction, the United States should take extra steps to make the majority of U.S. stored plutonium pits unusable in nuclear weapons and encourage Russia to make parallel steps with its stored pits.

Over the past eight years, major events and policy pronouncements have altered U.S. nuclear policy, whether in reality or in perception. In light of these changes, Congress has mandated that the new administration conduct a nuclear posture review. Although it is too early to know exactly where that review will head, then senator Obama, during the presidential campaign, offered a nuclear weapons policy that reiterated many George W. Bush administration objectives, such as securing loose weapons-usable nuclear material, preventing Iran from developing nuclear weapons, strengthening the nonproliferation regime, and maintaining a strong nuclear deterrent. But President Obama has departed substantially from the Bush administration in explicitly setting "a goal of a world without nuclear weapons, and pursu[ing] it."[7] In April 2009, he pledged that the United States "will take concrete steps toward a world without nuclear weapons" and would reduce nuclear stocks within the next four years.[8]

The Bush administration's nuclear posture review reaffirmed that nuclear weapons "play a critical role in the defense capabilities of the United States, its allies and friends."[9] One departure from previous reviews was an emphasis on planning based on capabilities rather than threats. Nonetheless, the review did single out six states—China, Libya, Iran, Iraq, Syria, and North Korea—as posing security concerns. Beijing objected to being placed on this list, but the review pointed out that because of "the combination of China's still developing strategic objectives and its ongoing modernization of its nuclear and nonnuclear forces, China . . . could be involved in an immediate or potential contingency." Although the review welcomed "a more cooperative relationship with Russia and a move away from the balance-of-terror policy framework," it underscored that "Russia's nuclear forces and programs, nevertheless, remain a concern. Russia faces many strategic problems around its periphery and its future course cannot be charted with certainty. U.S. planning must take this into account. In the event that U.S. relations with Russia significantly worsen in the future, the U.S. may need to revise its nuclear force levels and posture."

The review made another important change from previous policy in combining the former nuclear triad—the three legs of land-based

ballistic missiles, submarine-based ballistic missiles, and bombers—
with advanced conventional weapons and nonkinetic (information
warfare) capabilities to make up one leg of a new triad. The second leg
would include enhanced defensive capabilities, such as missile defense.
The third would consist of a responsive defense infrastructure to
respond relatively rapidly to security threats. According to officials who
worked on the review, these changes were intended to deemphasize the
role of nuclear weapons by showing that conventional weapons were a
fundamental part of defending the United States, even in the event of
a crisis involving nuclear weapons. Many officials also wanted to erect
a firewall between conventional and nuclear weapons. Critics raised
alarm that the policy put forward in the review would actually blur this
line. The Task Force believes that the George W. Bush administration
did not clearly and effectively communicate its intentions of its nuclear
posture review and that the administration should have published an
unclassified version. The Task Force urges the Obama administration
to make the effort, through briefings by senior officials and publication
of an unclassified version of the forthcoming nuclear posture review, to
explain to the American public and foreign audiences the purposes of
U.S. nuclear weapons posture. The 2006 British White Paper on Trident replacement would provide an excellent model.[10]

Compounding the perception problem was the review's discussion
of the need for a robust nuclear earth penetrator (RNEP) and other
possible new nuclear capabilities. Proponents claimed that the RNEP
would be capable of destroying hardened and deeply buried bunkers,
though it is not clear whether it in fact is capable of doing so. They
argued that the RNEP therefore had the potential to strengthen deterrence in certain scenarios by holding at risk an adversary's arsenal of
weapons of mass destruction (WMD).

Critics saw these possible developments as increasing the salience
of nuclear arms at a time when the United States would benefit from
raising the threshold of nuclear use, and expressed concern that the
RNEP, if used, would also create massive amounts of radioactive fallout. Many of the critics argued that the United States did not need the
RNEP because it had already developed the B61 mod 11 bomb during
the Clinton administration. The B61 mod 11 has a hardened bomb casing
to allow penetration in frozen soil; RNEP was intended to extend this
technology to allow similar penetration in rock. The George W. Bush
administration was building on the B61 mod 11 effort to explore a more

effective way of penetrating hard rock and simultaneously reducing the amount of fallout. But independent experts have cast significant doubt on the argument that the fallout would be limited.[11] Congress voted against appropriating money for these weapons.

A separate issue of whether to fund replacement strategic warheads has now surfaced in the debate about the future of the U.S. nuclear arsenal. Concerns about the message that replacement warheads—even if they are not tested—would send to other states continue. The Task Force believes that the Obama administration should undertake a detailed analysis of the proposed replacement warheads, with emphasis on the political and military costs and benefits. Although the Office of Management and Budget did not include funding for replacement warheads in the administration's budget request in early 2009, the administration will face a decision on replacement warheads later in its term.

FOREIGN GOVERNMENTS' PERCEPTIONS OF U.S. NUCLEAR WEAPONS POSTURE AND POLICY

The best way to understand how foreign governments perceive U.S. nuclear weapons policy and posture is to talk and listen to officials and analysts from other countries. Fortunately, in recent years, two studies have done just that. For a December 2006 study, Lewis Dunn, Gregory Giles, Jeffrey Larsen, and Thomas Skypek interviewed up to one hundred foreign officials and analysts about their views on U.S. nuclear policy and posture.[12] More recently, in 2008, Deepti Choubey interviewed dozens of officials in sixteen nonnuclear weapon states to determine their views on the potential for new nuclear bargains.[13] Both studies highlight the prevailing view among nonnuclear weapon states that the United States is not seriously following through on its nuclear disarmament pledge under the Nonproliferation Treaty. The studies also point out that progress toward disarmament, even if abolition is not attainable, would shore up allies' support for a stronger nonproliferation regime. On the other hand, these studies point out that these same allies view U.S. extended nuclear deterrence commitments—which would commit the United States to come to the defense of allies under possible nuclear attack—as an important aspect of their security.

The studies show that many foreign officials believe that the United States may be making nuclear weapons more usable as tools of war fighting. Interviewed officials in nonnuclear weapon states oppose U.S. development of new types of nuclear weapons, such as new nuclear earth penetrators or weapons with low nuclear yields, which they argue may blur the distinction between conventional and nuclear weapons.[14] The Task Force strongly urges the new administration to be transparent about U.S. decisions on nuclear policy, to bolster U.S. public diplomacy, and to listen carefully to the views of allies and other nonnuclear weapon states.

THE PURPOSES OF U.S. NUCLEAR WEAPONS

Has the transformed strategic landscape since the end of the Cold War reduced or altered the utility of U.S. nuclear weapons? Can advanced conventional weapons substitute for most, or perhaps all, nuclear military missions? Do U.S. allies still require an umbrella of extended nuclear deterrence from the United States? Must threats from chemical and biological weapons be deterred by nuclear weapons? Are nuclear weapons essential for the United States to maintain its global leadership role? The report examines these questions by assessing the following potential purposes for U.S. nuclear weapons: to deter use of other nuclear weapons against the United States, its military forces, and its allies; to deter use of chemical and biological weapons; to prevent defeat in a conventional war and deter conventional war between major powers; and to guard against blackmail by other nuclear-armed states and help preserve U.S. military capability to project power.

NUCLEAR DETERRENCE

U.S. nuclear weapons act as a deterrent force because American leaders can threaten to launch them in response to nuclear attacks against U.S. territory or military forces. In addition, the United States has leadership responsibilities in helping assure the security of many of its allies—for example, members of the North Atlantic Treaty Organization (NATO) alliance, Australia, Japan, and South Korea. Part of this security assurance involves protection against nuclear attack. U.S. nuclear weapons are one facet of multilayered defenses that include diplomacy, economic support, and conventional military forces to deter attacks and protect allies in the event of an attack. Without this assurance, some states currently under this nuclear umbrella may decide in the future to develop their own nuclear arms.

Most U.S. allies tend to be strong proponents for reducing the salience of nuclear weapons. At first glance, this stance might strike some observers as counterintuitive, as these states depend, in part, on these arms for their security. Japan represents an exemplar of this view. Long-standing Japanese policy strongly supports what it calls the three nuclear security pillars: pursuing nuclear disarmament, strengthening the nonproliferation regime, and ensuring continued and expanded use of peaceful nuclear energy. On the one hand, Tokyo is one of the strongest advocates for nuclear disarmament, but on the other, it relies on U.S. nuclear arms for protection. Japanese leaders believe that the long-term sustainability of the nonproliferation regime depends on the nuclear weapon states following through on their commitments to pursue disarmament. Nonetheless, some Japanese officials have expressed concern about whether U.S. nuclear posture provides an effective umbrella for Japan, especially in regard to China. Moreover, only a few years ago, before taking office, Japanese Prime Minister Taro Aso advocated that Japan debate the option of developing nuclear weapons.

In the NATO context, individual member states have mixed views about stationing U.S. short-range nuclear forces in some European NATO states. The February 2008 U.S. Air Force report pointing out security concerns of the basing of some of these forces prompted some European politicians to call for these weapons to be removed from Europe.[15] Other allied leaders, however, have reiterated their commitment to basing such weapons in their countries. Since the end of the Cold War, NATO's nuclear forces have shifted their doctrine from flexible response in war fighting and escalation control to one in which "the fundamental purpose of the nuclear forces" is "political: to preserve and prevent coercion." According to the same 2008 fact sheet, "NATO's nuclear forces contribute to European peace and stability by underscoring the irrationality of a major war in the Euro-Atlantic region." The fact sheet also notes that "at the same time, the dramatic changes in the security environment since the Cold War have allowed NATO to undertake equally dramatic reductions in its nuclear posture and in its reliance on nuclear weapons."[16] The Task Force agrees.

The Task Force believes that as long as U.S. alliance partners face the possibility of nuclear threats, the United States will have to retain enough nuclear arms to deter such threats. Determining an adequate quantity depends on developing threat assessments with allies and frequent consultation with them about their defense needs.

CHEMICAL AND BIOLOGICAL WEAPONS DETERRENCE

Although U.S. law includes nuclear, biological, and chemical weapons in the definition of weapons of mass destruction, these three classes of weapons vary considerably in their destructive capacities. All experts agree that nuclear weapons are undoubtedly weapons of mass destruction. There is less agreement, however, about whether to categorize all chemical and biological weapons as WMD. Chemical weapons have been used in warfare and in attacks on civilian populations: Iraqi president Saddam Hussein's chemical attack in 1988 that massacred Kurds in Halabja, for example. But to kill many people, relatively large numbers of chemical weapons would be needed to cause the level of destruction from a single nuclear weapon. In contrast, some experts believe that biological weapons could result in the deaths of hundreds of thousands of people and, under some circumstances, rival nuclear weapons in their ability to cause destruction.

International conventions outlaw chemical and biological weapons, but not nuclear weapons. Some states, however, such as Iran, North Korea, and Syria, are believed to have stockpiled these illicit arms despite such bans. Stopping such stockpiling is daunting partly because of the lack of verification provisions in the Biological Weapons and Toxins Convention and the dual-use potential of many biological and chemical techniques in industry. Because of this proliferation threat and because the United States has renounced chemical and biological weapons, U.S. leaders have considered using nuclear deterrence to prevent adversaries from using these weapons but have not explicitly threatened to do so.

Instead, U.S. leaders have practiced "calculated ambiguity" when crafting statements to foes armed with chemical and biological munitions. An oft-cited example is the letter Secretary of State James Baker delivered on January 9, 1991, from President George H.W. Bush to Iraqi deputy prime minister Tariq Aziz, stating that "the United States will not tolerate the use of chemical or biological weapons or the destruction of Kuwait's oil fields and installations. Further, you will be held directly responsible for terrorist actions against any member of the coalition.

The American people would demand the strongest possible response. You and your country will pay a terrible price if you order unconscionable acts of this sort." Note that the president's letter did not explicitly mention the use of nuclear weapons, but did not rule it out either.

The use of calculated ambiguity continued under the Clinton administration. In March 1996 in congressional testimony, Secretary of Defense William Perry (a chair of this Task Force) said, "For obvious reasons, we choose not to specify in detail what responses we would make to a chemical attack. However, as we stated during the Gulf War, if any country were foolish enough to use chemical weapons against the United States, the response will be 'absolutely overwhelming' and 'devastating.'"[17] One month later, Harold Smith, Perry's special assistant on nuclear, biological, and chemical programs, created a furor when he stated that the B61 nuclear bomb would be needed to destroy the suspected chemical weapons plant in Tarhunah, Libya. This mention of specific nuclear targeting of a suspected chemical weapons plant ran counter to the policy of calculated ambiguity, and forced the Pentagon to issue a statement that "there is no consideration of using nuclear weapons" against that plant.[18]

The Task Force believes that the policy of calculated ambiguity, in which U.S. officials have neither explicitly threatened nor ruled out the use of nuclear weapons in response to an adversary's use of chemical or biological weapons, continues to serve U.S. interests and notes that for plausible circumstances Washington should not have to resort to nuclear weapons to deter or respond to chemical or biological attacks.

CONVENTIONAL MILITARY THREATS

During much of the Cold War, the United States and NATO confronted quantitatively superior conventional forces fielded by the Soviet Union and the Warsaw Pact. To counter this threat, the United States developed strategic and battlefield nuclear weapons and war plans with options for first use of these weapons, massive retaliation in response to a nuclear attack, as well as relatively limited nuclear attacks. This threat diminished with the end of the Cold War. Today, the United States has the world's most powerful conventional military. More important, in terms of power projection, the U.S. military can relatively rapidly cover every point on the globe. Furthermore, no conventionally armed opponent now or in the foreseeable future could conquer the United States.

The United States does not currently need nuclear weapons to compensate for conventional military inferiority or to deter conventional
attacks against U.S. territory or against its allies. But because of U.S.
conventional superiority, other states may perceive the need to compensate for their relative weakness by acquiring nuclear weapons or at
least the capability to make such weapons as a way to deter the United
States from intervening on their territories.

NUCLEAR BLACKMAIL

Consider a world in which the United States has the same global leadership responsibilities it now has, but does not have nuclear arms, though
at least one adversary or potential adversary does. U.S. leaders would
then constantly remain concerned about coercion from that state. The
United States would not have the same power projection capabilities it
currently enjoys.

The Task Force believes that as long as the United States wants to
maintain its global leadership, it will need enough nuclear arms to prevent nuclear blackmail from other nuclear-armed states. Determining
what number and types of arms are adequate depends on geopolitical
dynamics and, ultimately, on U.S. leadership in reducing nuclear dangers and addressing other states' security concerns.

NUCLEAR ABOLITION AND THE RECENT
POLITICAL AND FOREIGN POLICY DEBATES

Recent debate among U.S. foreign policy experts and the presidential
candidates on reexamining nuclear abolition constitutes one of the
motivations for this report. In particular, three *Wall Street Journal* op-eds
published since January 2007 have renewed the debate about nuclear
disarmament.[19] During last year's presidential campaign, both Repub-
lican nominee Senator John McCain and Democratic nominee Senator Barack Obama spoke about the interrelated aspects of the vision
of a world free of nuclear weapons, the U.S. deterrent force, America's
security commitments to its allies, and further actions to prevent proliferation, indicating a bipartisan commitment to this issue.

On May 27, 2008, Senator McCain said:

A quarter of a century ago, President Ronald Reagan declared, "our dream is to see the day when nuclear weapons will be banished from the face of the Earth." That is my dream, too. It is a distant and difficult goal. And we must proceed toward it prudently and pragmatically, and with a focused concern for our security and the security of allies who depend on us. But the Cold War ended almost twenty years ago, and the time has come to take further measures to reduce dramatically the number of nuclear weapons in the world's arsenals. It is time for the United States to show the kind of leadership the world expects from us, in the tradition of American presidents who worked to reduce the nuclear threat to mankind.

On July 15, 2008, Senator Obama said:

> It's time to send a clear message: America seeks a world with no nuclear weapons. As long as nuclear weapons exist, we must retain a strong deterrent. But instead of threatening to kick them out of the G8, we need to work with Russia to take U.S. and Russian ballistic missiles off hair-trigger alert; to dramatically reduce the stockpiles of our nuclear weapons and material; to seek a global ban on the production of fissile material for weapons; and to expand the U.S.-Russian ban on intermediate-range missiles so that the agreement is global. By keeping our commitment under the Nonproliferation Treaty, we'll be in a better position to press nations like North Korea and Iran to keep theirs. In particular, it will give us more credibility and leverage in dealing with Iran.

Notably, the United States has a treaty obligation to pursue nuclear disarmament as well as general and complete disarmament, but there is no commitment for exactly when to achieve nuclear abolition. As a party to the 1970 Nuclear Nonproliferation Treaty, the United States has committed to Article VI of this treaty, as follows: "Each of the Parties to the Treaty undertakes to pursue negotiations in good faith on effective measures relating to cessation of the nuclear arms race at an early date and to nuclear disarmament, and on a Treaty on general and complete disarmament under strict and effective international control."

Task Force members have differing views on the feasibility or even desirability of achieving the global elimination of nuclear weapons, but all agree that, if feasible, abolition will likely require decades to accomplish. The Task Force believes that reenergized global actions to prevent nuclear proliferation and nuclear terrorism are needed to lessen those dangers. Further, the Task Force observes that many allies believe (though some do not) that supporting the goal of nuclear elimination helps build the international trust and broad cooperation required to effectively stem the increasing dangers of nuclear proliferation and nuclear terrorism. In sum, supporting the long-term goal of nuclear disarmament may be necessary to mobilize widespread support for the short-term actions needed to further reduce nuclear dangers.

This report focuses on the near-term steps for U.S. nuclear policy and posture. Depending on the outcome of these steps, a pathway for nuclear abolition may become feasible, but it should be revisited as the near-term steps are achieved.

THE ROAD AHEAD FOR U.S. NUCLEAR WEAPONS POLICY

As a starting point for forming more effective U.S. nuclear policies, the United States needs to understand the concerns of its allies, as well as of Russia and China. Although bilateral and multilateral cooperation are important for nuclear risk reduction strategies, the United States can and should continue to take unilateral actions, such as implementing best security practices over its nuclear weapons and fissile material and reducing the amounts of weapons and material it determines are excess to its defense needs. Nonetheless, any major restructuring of the U.S. nuclear posture hinges on strategic dialogue with Russia and, eventually, with China. Before undertaking these dialogues, the United States itself has to understand its strategic objectives with respect to nuclear policy and posture and the interconnectedness to other states' security objectives.

In the next chapter, the report provides an overview of the current security environment relevant for U.S. nuclear policy. After this analysis, the report considers U.S. relations with other nuclear-armed states, which fundamentally shape the strategies of preventing proliferation and securing nuclear weapons. Of these relationships, the report pays special attention to the U.S.-Russia nuclear agenda. The U.S.-China strategic relationship will also have growing importance in the coming years; consequently, the report devotes the following chapter to examining next steps in that relationship.

The report then focuses on the core strategies of preventing proliferation and securing and reducing nuclear weapons and weapons-usable materials. In those chapters, the report considers multilateral nuclear fuel assurances, best security practices, the Comprehensive Test Ban Treaty, bans on fissile material production, the transformation of the U.S. nuclear weapons complex, reductions in nuclear weapons, and the composition of U.S. nuclear forces. The Task Force emphasizes that these strategies must support the primary objective of preventing the use of nuclear weapons by states or nonstate actors. The report concludes with recommendations for guiding the new president in shaping U.S. nuclear posture and policy to more effectively prevent the use of nuclear weapons.

The New Security Environment

In the early 1990s, U.S. leaders saw opportunities and perils emerge out of the fall of the Soviet Union. The former Eastern Bloc countries and the Soviet successor states offered an enlargement of "the family of nations now committed to the pursuit of democratic institutions, the expansion of free markets, the peaceful settlement of conflict and the promotion of collective security," as then national security adviser Anthony Lake observed. However, Lake also warned that U.S. policy "must face the reality of recalcitrant and outlaw states that not only choose to remain outside the family but also assault its basic values."[20]

Senator McCain more recently cautioned that a nuclear-empowered Iran "would be even more willing and able to sponsor terrorist attacks against any perceived enemy, including the United States and Israel, or even to pass nuclear materials to one of its allied terrorist networks."[21] A related concern is that the leaders of these states may not be as prone to deterrence as the Soviet Union was during the Cold War.

Concerns about constraints on American power projection and increased regional instability have thus shaped U.S. policy toward emerging nuclear-capable states. The United States has pursued unilateral and multilateral means of diplomacy, nonproliferation, counterproliferation, and military preparedness, including missile defenses, to try to prevent such states from acquiring WMD or to defend against their use of such weapons.

RUSSIA

Although Russia is no longer an enemy, and the United States has substantially reduced its number of deployed and stockpiled warheads, thousands of nuclear weapons remain in the U.S. and Russian arsenals. The likelihood of intentional war with Russia has substantially decreased since the demise of the Soviet Union, but the risk of miscalculation persists. Because this latent threat is the only man-made danger that can cause the immediate destruction of the United States, the time is long overdue to reexamine whether the United States and Russia can agree to further reduce the risk of nuclear conflict through better situational awareness of their nuclear postures and better communication about nuclear policy and decision making regarding their nuclear arsenals. Although reducing nuclear arms would not necessarily decrease the risk of miscalculation, it is an important part of the nuclear arms control agenda.

This agenda will, however, have to contend with other issues, which have the potential to return the United States and Russia to an adversarial relationship. Tensions over NATO enlargement, the 2008 Georgia-Russia armed conflict, and proposed U.S. missile defense deployments in the Czech Republic and Poland are three of the most vexing issues that have increased tensions between the United States and Russia. The conflict with Georgia in particular has raised concerns about the direction of Russian foreign policy. Nevertheless, Russian leaders generally welcome formal arms control talks. Negotiating a follow-on to the Strategic Arms Reduction Treaty (START)—set to expire in December 2009—will top this agenda.

The large Russian arsenal of short-range nuclear weapons is believed by many security experts to be more susceptible to theft or diversion than Russia's strategic weapons. Under the 1991 and 1992 pledges by U.S. president George H.W. Bush, Soviet president Mikhail Gorbachev, and Russian president Boris Yeltsin, Russia agreed to eliminate nuclear ground and naval forces. The United States pledged to reduce most of its short-range nuclear weapon systems and has subsequently dismantled warheads associated with these systems. There are concerns that Russia did not completely fulfill these dismantlement pledges, according to Stephen Rademaker, then acting assistant secretary of state for international nonproliferation.[22] Notably, these pledges, known as the Presidential Nuclear Initiatives, were not accompanied by any verification provisions. The totality of the issues briefly discussed here underscores the fundamental importance of U.S.-Russia relations, which are explored in detail in the next chapter.

CHINA

After decades of remaining outside the formal nonproliferation regime, China joined the Nonproliferation Treaty in 1992 and has since been trying to improve its weak export controls against illicit transfers of technologies and materials that can fuel weapons of mass destruction programs. In parallel, China has been gradually modernizing and expanding its nuclear arsenal to buttress its minimal deterrent, in part hedging against the growth of the U.S. missile defense system and conventional strike capabilities. The primary objective is to preclude U.S. intervention if China uses force against Taiwan, in response, for example, to a possible Taiwanese move to declare formal independence from China, or to a Chinese decision to incorporate Taiwan into the mainland by force. The most plausible—indeed, perhaps the only plausible—military threat to the United States from China emanates from a potential confrontation over Taiwan and underscores the mutual interest China and the United States share in continuing to manage the Taiwan issue well. U.S.-China relations are explored in more detail in a later chapter.

IRAN AND NORTH KOREA

Presently, the two regions of greatest concern with regard to nuclear weapons capabilities are Northeast Asia, where North Korea has developed nuclear weapons programs, and the Middle East, where Iran has been developing the breakout capability for making nuclear weapons. North Korea has produced a small stockpile of plutonium it says it has used to build a small arsenal of first-generation nuclear bombs. It tested a nuclear device that produced a small explosive yield in October 2006, and claimed earlier this year that it had produced nuclear weapons from its plutonium stockpile.[23] Throughout much of 2008, North Korea made significant progress on disabling its ability to make additional plutonium for bombs and had agreed to dismantle its nuclear weapons programs. The United States will need to strengthen the resolve of the six-party coalition, which also includes China, Japan, Russia, and South Korea, to keep any dismantlement on track. It will have to devote considerable effort to managing competing interests among coalition members. The United States has faced difficulties when working with North Korea. Significant challenges will confront the new administration in sustaining efforts toward dismantling North Korea's nuclear weapons programs and verifying this dismantlement. Pyongyang expelled U.S. nuclear experts and international inspectors in April 2009, a response to UN Security Council condemnation of North Korea's test of a long-range rocket that same month.

Iran poses perhaps the toughest problem for the nuclear nonprolif-eration regime because it is acquiring a latent capability to make nuclear weapons under the guise of a civilian uranium enrichment program. U.S. and allied efforts to convince Iran to suspend this program have been unsuccessful. What is more, several states in the Middle East have expressed an interest—partly in response to Iran's growing capabil-ity—in developing peaceful nuclear power programs. Although they are likely many years away from acquiring the technologies to make weapons-usable nuclear material, strategic surprises could occur. For example, according to the U.S. government, Syria was building a reac-tor with North Korean assistance that would have had the capacity to produce plutonium when operational; Israel bombed the construction site on September 6, 2007.

According to the November 2007 U.S. National Intelligence Esti-mate, the National Intelligence Council has judged "with moderate confidence that the earliest possible date Iran would be technically capable of producing enough [highly enriched uranium] for a weapon is late 2009, but that this is very unlikely" and that "with moderate confi-dence Iran probably would be technically capable of producing enough HEU for a weapon sometime during the 2010–2015 time frame.. . . All [intelligence] agencies recognize the possibility that this capability may not be attained until *after* 2015."[24] Concern exists about a military component to Iran's civilian nuclear program. Notably, in a November 2008 report, the director general of the International Atomic Energy Agency (IAEA) stated that "a number of outstanding issues . . . give rise to concerns and need to be clarified to exclude the existence of possible military dimensions" to the Iranian nuclear program.[25] The IAEA's February 2009 report criticized Iran for noncooperation.[26]

These IAEA reports emphasize the importance of Iran's providing the information and access to personnel and facilities needed to resolve these concerns. Even if the IAEA obtains clarity about past violations, Iran still has the obligation to make clear its plans for current and pos-sible future nuclear facilities and, most important, to meet its respon-sibility to not seek to acquire nuclear weapons. Iran's nuclear program poses the most significant challenge to strengthening the rules-based nonproliferation regime and preventing a nuclear arms race in the Middle East. (A later chapter presents an analysis of needed efforts to prevent further nuclear proliferation.)

NONSTATE ACTORS

The most likely scenario for the detonation of a nuclear weapon involves nonstate actors seeking nuclear explosives. Traditional nuclear deterrence would most probably not work against stateless terrorists, given that they do not have a national territory that can be targeted. This type of deterrence, however, might be relevant against their state sponsors, if any.

Mass casualty terrorism has increased in the past three decades. Although some terrorist groups have acquired and used chemical and biological weapons, no group is yet known to have acquired nuclear weapons or significant amounts of nuclear weapons-usable materials. Al-Qaeda, however, has expressed this intent, and many experts fear that it would not hesitate to detonate such weapons. To respond to this threat, the United States has been increasing its efforts to reduce and secure nuclear weapons and weapons-usable nuclear materials and to interdict nuclear weapons or materials in transit before they reach the United States. Blocking access in this way is a preventive measure against nuclear terrorism, given that terrorist groups do not have the ability now or in the foreseeable future to make highly enriched uranium or plutonium—the two fissile materials most usable for nuclear weapons.

States, particularly those that have been state sponsors of terrorism, could provide weapons-usable fissile materials directly to terrorist groups. Thus, a complementary area of response is to hold complicit states accountable for the actions of such groups.[27] States might also be held accountable for failing to secure their nuclear weapons and weapons-usable materials. Forensics can help trace or attribute a nuclear weapon—either before or after detonation—to its place of origin, though its results may not be reliable enough to function as actionable evidence. The Task Force recognizes that enforcing states' accountability of nuclear weapons and weapons-usable materials is fraught with political and technical challenges, but it is nonetheless important.

INDIA AND PAKISTAN

India and Pakistan have presented several challenges to preventing the use and further acquisition of nuclear weapons and the technologies used to make those weapons. Although these countries have always remained outside the NPT, and thus have not violated international law in acquiring nuclear weapons, their intense rivalry and Pakistan's conventional military inferiority with respect to India have raised the threat of nuclear weapons use on the state-to-state level. Continual waves of political instability in Pakistan and the presence of nuclear-motivated terrorists in both Pakistan and Afghanistan have raised the risk of nonstate actors acquiring and using nuclear weapons. Numerous conventional terrorist attacks in India and Pakistan and the festering, unresolved status of Kashmir have also increased the probability of these countries fighting a conventional war that could escalate to nuclear weapons use.

Although Pakistan has reportedly improved the security of its nuclear weapons, these efforts are not complete—it still lacks adequate controls on its nuclear weapons-usable technologies, such as uranium enrichment.[28] Abdul Qadeer Khan, the leader of Pakistan's uranium enrichment program, headed a nuclear black market that distributed uranium enrichment equipment and knowledge to Iran, Libya, and North Korea. Khan's associates also gave Libya designs for a nuclear weapon. Electronic copies found on computers in Dubai and Switzerland suggest, furthermore, that these designs may have leaked to other countries interested in acquiring nuclear weapons, or even to terrorist groups. This black market operated from at least the late 1980s to late 2003, and its remnants may still be in operation. And with his release from house arrest in February 2009, Khan may be able to renew his involvement in the market, although Islamabad has pledged to enact better controls over nuclear technologies.

These are daunting challenges, but the United States has leverage over both India and Pakistan. The United States has designated Pakistan a major non-NATO ally and in recent years has provided billions of dollars of aid to the country. The previous administration also concluded a civilian nuclear cooperation deal with India, ending more than thirty years of Indian isolation from the global commercial nuclear market. One of the primary motivations behind the deal was to further cement relationships between the world's oldest democracy, the United

States, and the world's largest democracy, India. The United States has a clear interest in redoubling diplomatic and security assistance efforts to leverage and build on existing ties with both India and Pakistan in order to reduce the risk of nuclear weapons use and leakage of nuclear weapons, technologies, and materials. A later chapter discusses best nuclear security practices that the United States can help implement in India and Pakistan.

U.S.-Russia Relations

Throughout much of the Cold War, mutual self-interest motivated the United States and the Soviet Union to pursue formal arms control agreements with the aim of limiting the nuclear arms race, promoting strategic stability, and avoiding mutual destruction in a nuclear war. They concluded agreements such as the Anti-Ballistic Missile (ABM) Treaty, the Intermediate-Range Nuclear Forces (INF) Treaty, and the Strategic Arms Reduction Treaty. Since the early 1990s, however, the U.S. approach to arms control with Russia has evolved. Objecting to formal arms control agreements as relics of the Cold War inconsistent with the new strategic relationship the United States sought to forge with the Russian Federation, the George W. Bush administration emphasized flexibility in force deployment, simplified verification measures, and negotiations that could be concluded in months, not years. Indeed, within its first year, the Bush administration reached agreement with Russia on the 2002 Strategic Offensive Reductions Treaty, which relied on START's verification provisions and allowed both sides considerable flexibility to determine their respective force structures. SORT expires on December 31, 2012; START expires on December 5, 2009, unless extended according to its own provisions.

Although these impending deadlines are important and demand attention, they arise in the context of underlying tensions in the U.S.-Russia relationship. The long-term implications of the August 2008 armed conflict between Russia and Georgia, perceived Western encroachment into Russia's traditional spheres of influence, Russian opposition to NATO enlargement to include former Soviet states such as Georgia and Ukraine, Russia's conventional military inferiority with respect to the United States and NATO, Russian resistance to U.S. missile defense deployment in eastern and central Europe, concerns about the vitality of the Russian nuclear deterrent, and increasingly divergent attitudes toward arms control have stymied progress on further bilateral nuclear arms reductions. However, the change in administrations provides an opportunity to put the U.S.-Russia relationship on a new footing. Vice President Joseph R. Biden Jr. said in February 2009, "It is time to press the reset button and to revisit the many areas where we can and should be working together with Russia."[29] Specifically, he emphasized cooperation with Russia "to secure loose nuclear weapons and materials to prevent their spread, to renew the verification procedures in the START Treaty, and then go beyond existing treaties to negotiate deeper cuts in both our arsenals. The United States and Russia have a special obligation to lead the international effort to reduce the number of nuclear weapons in the world."[30] In April 2009, President Barack Obama reinforced this commitment when he and Russian president Dmitry Medvedev both pledged to further reduce their nuclear arsenals.

This chapter examines the opportunities for renewed cooperation with Russia on nuclear security, including the following:

- preserving the legal foundation for verification underpinning SORT and maintaining transparency and predictability for U.S. and Russian strategic nuclear forces while negotiating deeper nuclear arms reductions below the START and SORT levels;

- creating improved crisis stability and situational awareness of each side's nuclear and missile capabilities, and mutually exploring the implications for crisis stability of advanced conventional weapons such as the proposal for conventionally armed Trident missiles;

- countering nuclear and missile proliferation threats with attention to the Iranian nuclear and missile programs;

- determining whether the United States and Russia can develop a cooperative missile defense program;

- making further reductions in weapons-usable fissile material by converting it to nonweapons-usable forms such as nuclear reactor fuel;

- transitioning cooperative threat reduction programs from assistance programs into true partnerships; and

- discussing the next steps in nuclear arms reductions involving other nuclear-armed states.

NUCLEAR FORCES AND FORCE STRUCTURE

U.S.-Russia arms control agreements have been invaluable in help-ing stabilize strategic relations, developing a shared understanding of activities involving nuclear weapons, and lending predictability to reductions in American and Russian strategic nuclear forces. Both sides have expressed interest in renewing arms control negotiations. The Task Force welcomes the opportunity to renew arms control talks and approves of a U.S.-Russia dialogue toward deeper reductions in their arsenals.

The two nuclear arms control agreements currently in force are START and SORT. Both have advantages and disadvantages. START provides rigorous verification measures, some of which the United States and Russia now regard as overly burdensome, but which also provide a high degree of transparency and confidence about each side's nuclear forces. By contrast, SORT has no verification require-ments because it was negotiated with the understanding that START would remain in force. START limits the number and type of strate-gic nuclear delivery vehicles each side can have, and contains count-ing rules that attribute specific numbers of warheads to each type of strategic nuclear delivery vehicle. SORT, on the other hand, limits only the number of "strategic nuclear warheads," a term not defined in the treaty, which leaves each side the freedom both to define for itself what warheads are limited by the treaty and to choose the number and type of delivery vehicles to carry those warheads. SORT thus pro-vides each side with greater flexibility to determine the makeup of its strategic force structure. The United States has determined that only operationally deployed warheads are limited by SORT, referring to those warheads actually deployed on operational delivery vehicles or at bomber bases ready for such deployment. SORT thus permits an unrestricted number of warheads to remain in reserve and potentially available for rapid and undetected uploading on strategic delivery vehicles that have the capacity to carry additional warheads. Neither treaty requires actual dismantlement of warheads; however, START, in contrast to SORT, does mandate the destruction of some launchers and delivery vehicles. The data exchange required by START provides a valuable source of information on the status of each side's strategic nuclear forces.

In a joint statement released on April 1, 2009, Russian president Medvedev and U.S. president Obama agreed to begin bilateral negotiations to create a new, comprehensive, legally binding agreement to replace START. The new agreement will deal with the reduction and limitation of strategic forces, reduce these levels below SORT requirements, and include START-derived verification measures. Both parties have committed to conclude this agreement before START expires in December 2009.

Success in negotiating a follow-on bilateral arms control treaty with Russia will require clarity about the long-term strategic visions of both the United States and Russia. As part of a reinvigorated strategic dialogue, both countries should explore the geopolitical implications of deeper reductions and changes in nuclear force posture: Do the United States and Russia have a common view of the global implications of their disarmament actions, given that many states link the vitality of the nonproliferation regime to progress in U.S.-Russia nuclear arms reductions? What plans does each side have for future nuclear force modernization? To what extent will those plans either shape, or be shaped by, the bilateral agreements they reach? With respect to much deeper nuclear reductions, does Russia view its status as a nuclear superpower as necessary to maintaining its stature globally? How much does Russia depend on its nuclear weapons for deterrence in light of the post–Cold War deterioration of its conventional forces? How do proposed Russian plans for military modernization affect this dependence?

Russia's Soviet-legacy nuclear forces are aging and nearing the end of their design life. Also, many of its multiple independently targetable reentry vehicle (MIRV) ICBMs are facing obsolescence by 2015. To compensate for these declining forces, Russia has been slowly deploying some modern single-warhead Topol-M ICBMs (NATO designation SS-27) and has been developing a three-warhead variant of this system that, according to START rules, would qualify as a new type and thus be prohibited. The Topol-M missiles are also reported to have enhanced features to penetrate U.S. missile defenses.[31] Russia, however, has not been able to build and deploy enough Topol-Ms to replace all the missiles nearing retirement. Therefore, without the capacity to produce additional missiles more quickly and to deploy the new MIRVed variant, the Russian ICBM force will descend rapidly along its current downward trajectory in the coming seven years and beyond.

COUNCIL *on* FOREIGN RELATIONS

58 East 68th Street, New York, New York 10065
tel 212.434.9400 fax 212.434.9800 www.cfr.org

June 15, 2009

The Honorable Sandy Louise Vogelgesang
9009 Charred Oak Dr
Bethesda, MD 20817-1923

Dear Dr. Vogelgesang:

As chairs of the effort, we are pleased to share with you a new Independent Task Force report on U.S. nuclear weapons policy sponsored by the Council on Foreign Relations.

While President Obama has called for the eventual global abolition of nuclear weapons, they will remain a fundamental element of U.S. national security in the near term. This Task Force report makes recommendations, therefore, on how to ensure the safety, security, and reliability of the U.S. deterrent nuclear force. Taking stock of the new security environment, the report also puts forth measures to prevent nuclear terrorism and strengthen the nuclear nonproliferation regime.

The report is also available online at CFR.org. We hope you will find it of interest.

Sincerely,

Bill Perry and Brent Scowcroft
Chairs

Enclosure

Like the ICBMs, the Russian navy's submarine force has declined with the retirement of older ballistic missile submarines (SSBNs) and even many of the more modern Delta-class and Typhoon-class SSBNs. Nonetheless, after many years of development, the newest Russian SSBN completed last April and a new submarine-launched ballistic missile (SLBM) is being developed for it. However, Russia will likely need many years to build enough of these replacement Borey-class submarines to compensate for older submarine retirements. Moreover, the existing submarine fleet rarely goes on patrols; its survivability depends on the receipt of strategic warning. Similarly, Russia's strategic bombers are decades-old, and the Russian military has begun to slowly modernize its bomber fleet.

Russian strategic nuclear forces would likely decline by 2012 to no more than two thousand total deployed warheads, with roughly six hundred on ICBMs (many of them single-warhead systems), six hundred on SLBMs, and eight hundred on strategic bombers. These forces would meet the SORT limits. Nevertheless, this downward trajectory in overall Russian strategic nuclear force levels helps explain Russia's interest in negotiating with the United States a legally binding treaty with lower limits on strategic nuclear forces. Moreover, to maintain rough parity with the United States, Russia needs to deploy the new three-warhead variant of the SS-27 and therefore requires a modification of the START counting rules so that under a successor treaty this system would be permitted.

The Task Force believes that further strategic arms reductions would serve American and Russian interests, and that the two sides would benefit from a legally binding arms control agreement, but that it is premature to specify the goal number for weapon reductions. The Task Force also believes it is desirable to premise U.S.-Russia arms control negotiations on a shared understanding of each side's strategic vision.

In contrast to offensive strategic nuclear weapons and intermediate-range forces, Russia and the United States have never included short-range nuclear weapon delivery systems, such as nuclear-capable tactical aircraft and land- or sea-based nuclear-armed cruise missiles, in a formal arms control agreement. They did, however, each withdraw from deployment certain short-range nuclear weapons in the Presidential Nuclear Initiatives of 1991–92. The United States has far fewer short-range nuclear weapons than Russia. According to unofficial estimates, the United States has forward deployed a few hundred (all designed for delivery by dual-capable aircraft) in NATO states, whereas Russia may have several thousands of these types of weapons (in various states of readiness, reserve status, or awaiting dismantlement).[32] The Task Force believes that basing U.S. short-range nuclear weapons still has political value to some NATO countries, because removing them might raise political questions about the credibility of U.S. extended deterrence.

The small U.S. nuclear stockpile deployed in Europe still supports NATO political objectives and may help convince certain NATO allies not to build their own nuclear forces. The Task Force emphasizes that any changes in U.S. nonstrategic nuclear forces should be made only in close consultation with NATO allies. This European-based stockpile must be afforded the highest degree of physical security possible. A 2008 Defense Science Board report addressed this issue.[33]

The U.S. short-range weapons in Europe have been a perennial sore point for Russia. The large number of Russian short-range nuclear weapons have concerned nuclear security experts because of the possibility that some of these weapons could fall into the hands of terrorists or other malicious actors. A weapon-for-weapon trade between the United States and Russia is not credible for these shorter-range nuclear weapons because of the large disparity in the two countries' forces. The Task Force observes that Russia has a strong interest in taking further steps to reduce, secure, and consolidate these weapons to lessen the likelihood of loss of control.

CRISIS STABILITY AND SITUATIONAL AWARENESS

Even after the deep nuclear reductions that followed the end of the Cold War, the United States and Russia still keep thousands of nuclear weapons on a ready-launch posture. Although the countries have not officially targeted each other since U.S. president Bill Clinton and Russian president Boris Yeltsin signed a detargeting agreement in 1994, nuclear-armed missiles can be retargeted in a matter of minutes and there is no reliable way to verify the detargeted status.

Maintaining nuclear weapons on high alert or returning them to this status during a crisis could prompt rash actions at a time when restraint is most needed. If in such a situation one side became convinced of the other's intention to attack, it would have an incentive to limit the potential damage by preemptively destroying as many of the opponent's strategic nuclear weapons as possible, thus reducing the number of warheads that could detonate on its own territory. Submarines in port, bombers on the ground, mobile land-based missiles stored in garrisons, and multiple-warhead ICBMs in stationary silos are vulnerable weapon systems because they can be easily targeted. Single-warhead silo-based ballistic missiles, though vulnerable, do not invite preemptive attack because the perpetrator would expend more warheads than the number he would be able to destroy.

The ultimate measure to preventing damage limitation involves creating strategic forces not susceptible to preemptive attack. One driver of U.S. arms control policy in the Cold War was the goal of encouraging the Soviet Union to restructure its forces in stabilizing ways. The situation is further complicated by the fact that the same ability to launch ICBMs rapidly in advance of an attack (to limit damage) is also needed once an attack has begun (to conduct a retaliatory strike).

With respect to strategic stability, Russia and the United States present a study in contrasts. Russia has the majority of its strategically deployed warheads on ballistic missiles based in silos, though it keeps a small portion of its ballistic missiles on mobile systems that are seldom out of garrison.[34] Although Russia has approximately six hundred warheads assigned to submarines, its submarine force in recent years has not maintained continuous at-sea deployments. Even during the Cold War, however, the Russians generally discounted surprise attacks and assumed that a nuclear war would grow out of a conventional conflict. Keeping submarines ready in port preserves reactor core life—saving money—and appears to be a rational response from the Russian perspective. Because the United States can afford to do so, and because it has sought to guard against another Pearl Harbor–type surprise attack, it has the majority of its readily available strategic warheads on submarines and continuously keeps several submarines at sea. In sum, the United States has high confidence in its second-strike nuclear force and thus has a credible and reliable deterrent. Meanwhile, Russia has less confidence in being able to withstand a first strike under all the conceivable circumstances. Growing U.S. capabilities in precision-guided conventional munitions and U.S. proposals to deploy conventionally armed ballistic missiles on Trident submarines only increase Russian concerns. But even under the current conditions or based on worst-case assumptions about Russia's vulnerability, Russia would most likely have considerable second-strike nuclear forces to ensure its deterrent.

This assessment does not imply that the United States has nuclear primacy or dominance over Russia. Nonetheless, perceptions matter. The Task Force believes the United States needs to be transparent about its intentions and capabilities, including nuclear and advanced conventional weapons, to assure Russian officials that it neither has nor seeks nuclear dominance or primacy.

The Task Force also believes the United States and Russia have a mutual interest in improving situational awareness of each other's ballistic missile activities—specifically, to reduce the risk of strategic miscalculation and to increase confidence in each side's command and control over ballistic missile launches. Along these lines, the United States and Russia should implement the memorandum of understanding that President Bill Clinton and President Boris Yeltsin signed in September 1998 to establish the Joint Data Exchange Center, which was designed to provide an exchange of information derived from each side's missile launch warning systems on missile and space vehicle launches. The two countries have discussed forming this center for many years, but have yet to implement it.

MISSILE PROLIFERATION AND MISSILE DEFENSE

Another important issue for U.S.-Russia dialogue is missile defense. In 2002, the United States withdrew from the ABM Treaty, which had limited the numbers and locations of missile interceptors in a defense system, because it aimed to deploy a national missile defense system—focused on North Korea and Iran—that would go beyond the limitations of the treaty. The 2008 U.S.-Russia Sochi Declaration refers to continuing and intensifying dialogue on missile defense cooperation at both the bilateral and multilateral levels. In an additional statement released on April 1, 2009, presidents Obama and Medvedev acknowledged opportunities for cooperation on missile defense that will take into account joint assessments of missile threats and the relationship between offensive and defense arms. However, the issue remains a difficult one. Washington has pursued a missile defense system in the hope that it would both deter the development of nuclear weapons by states like Iran and protect the United States should such deterrence fail. In April 2009, President Obama affirmed that "as long as the threat from Iran persists, we will go forward with a missile defense system that is cost-effective and proven."[35]

Especially toxic for Russia is the question of deploying elements of a U.S. ballistic missile defense system in eastern and central Europe. The Bush administration favored a ground-based, long-range antimissile shield featuring ten ballistic missile interceptors in Poland and a large forward-based X-band radar in the Czech Republic. Russian officials are bothered by the political-military encroachment of the United States and NATO that these deployments in former Warsaw Pact states represent. In addition, Russia claims that such a system, because it can be upgraded, could gain the capacity to overwhelm a significant portion of the Russian nuclear deterrent. Some independent American scientists also point to concerns that the currently modest plans could expand to give the United States the capability to shoot down significant numbers of Russian ballistic missile warheads.[36]

Taking into account U.S. missile defense plans as publicly announced and Russian concerns about the proposed deployments, the Task Force offers the following guidance for the Obama administration:

- Delay missile defense deployments in Europe until the proposed system is determined to be technically viable.
- Link missile defense interceptor deployments and missile defense system architecture, the location and capabilities of these interceptors, and system capabilities such as range of operation to an assessment of the ballistic missile proliferation threat from Iran and North Korea.
- Include Russia and European allies in this threat assessment and reenergize U.S.-Russia-EU efforts to resolve the nuclear proliferation threat from Iran. (As President Obama already indicated in his February 2009 letter to President Medvedev, the proposed missile defense system would not be necessary if Moscow were to help stop Iran from developing long-range weapons and nuclear warheads.)
- Work with Russia on appropriate confidence-building measures to convince the Russians that their deterrent is not being undermined.
- Consult with Russia and European allies about U.S. missile defense proposals and seek to determine whether the United States and

Russia should build a cooperative missile defense. (Delays in deployment would also allow for a more serious dialogue about cooperative defenses and a joint assessment on the missile proliferation threat.)

Deeper nuclear arms reductions below the SORT limits may depend on U.S. willingness to substantially limit or even halt its national ballistic missile defense deployments, at least in Europe. The subject of missile defense has a global dimension, with significant ramifications outside the U.S.-Russia context. It is important to differentiate between theater missile defenses and the U.S. national missile defenses that have raised Russian and Chinese concerns. Theater defenses are more technically mature, provide force protection for U.S. troops and allies, and have served to reassure allies such as Israel and Japan. Notably for China, theater missile defense in East Asia has strategic ramifications.

SECURING AND REDUCING NUCLEAR MATERIALS

Connected to nuclear arms reductions is the security and reduction of weapons-usable nuclear materials. As warheads are dismantled, highly enriched uranium and plutonium are separated and become more vulnerable to theft or diversion unless strong security measures are in place. Converting HEU and plutonium into forms that are unusable in nuclear weapons is also important, because it demonstrates a practical step toward nuclear disarmament. It would also help achieve permanent risk reduction for these materials, which could be seized by terrorists.

For more than seventeen years, the United States has been assisting Russia and other former Soviet states in securing weapons-usable nuclear materials through a number of cooperative threat reduction programs. These programs have generally been praised as successful in increasing nuclear security in Russia and the former Soviet Union. The approximately $10 billion the United States has invested has provided for the dismantlement of hundreds of ballistic missiles, the deactivation of thousands of nuclear warheads, significant improvements in security of weapons and materials, and the repatriation of hundreds of kilograms of Russian-origin HEU.

During the 1990s, when Russia was in dire economic shape, it depended heavily on foreign security assistance. Once it began to benefit from high global oil and gas prices, a growing consensus emerged in the United States, including in the Congress, that Russia should assume greater financial responsibility for sustaining the nuclear security improvements gained with U.S. assistance. However, the current economic crisis renews concerns about Russia's ability to fund and prioritize such nuclear security projects. Russia's investments in nuclear security remain opaque. U.S. specialists indicate that Russian security culture and senior-level awareness of nuclear risks is neither well enough developed nor widespread enough to give confidence that Russia will provide robust budgets and strong oversight on nuclear security measures. Most of the planned Cooperative Threat Reduction (CTR) efforts in Russia have been completed, but their achievements need to be sustained over the long term. The challenge now, particularly in the current economic climate, is to transform the U.S.-Russia security relationship from one of assistance to one of real partnership and to ensure that Russia maintains security improvements in good working order once U.S. funding ends.

The Task Force believes that the United States has a strong interest in working with Russia to create an approach to nonproliferation cooperation that appropriately reflects both sides' interests, capacities, and responsibilities to secure and reduce nuclear weapons and materials.

One successful U.S.-Russia program was the Warhead Safety and Security Exchange (WSSX), which CTR did not cover. Implemented in 1994, the WSSX agreement sought to develop more effective counter–nuclear terrorism techniques, in addition to better safety and security of nuclear weapons. The United States and Russia should revitalize nuclear warhead safety and security programs through an umbrella agreement that would allow U.S. and Russian experts to work jointly to develop new technical approaches to arms control verification, nonproliferation, and counterterrorism.

Another successful nuclear risk reduction program is Megatons-to-Megawatts, through which Russia and the United States have agreed to convert five hundred metric tons of weapons-grade uranium from the Russian weapons program into low-enriched uranium (LEU) fuel for U.S. nuclear power plants. This material is equivalent to about twenty thousand bombs' worth of uranium. From 1994 to 2008, this program has converted about three hundred and fifty metric tons into nuclear fuel. This fuel has provided half of the fuel for U.S. nuclear power plants and thus generates about 10 percent of U.S. electricity needs. The conversion of the weapons-grade uranium has been paid for through commercial sales, totaling $12 billion, and not through taxpayer subsidies.[37] The program is scheduled for completion in 2013.

In May 2002, President Bush and President Putin formed an intergovernmental group to investigate how to build on this program. But the two sides did not reach agreement on a deal to significantly expand the program. Russia may have wanted to keep much, if not all, of its remaining HEU in reserve for its own use. In 2003, however, the United States explored Russia's interest in increasing the conversion rate from 30 to 31.5 tons annually, through an arrangement by which the United States would have placed the excess low enriched material in a strategic reserve. Congress declined to fund this proposal, however, on the basis of concerns about flooding the market with LEU. To obtain industry buy-in for a significant expansion of the program, some U.S. nuclear industry officials have proposed setting aside a reserve of fuel from excess HEU for a group of reactors that have yet to be built. This proposal would promote the growth of more nuclear power plants in the United States and serve nonproliferation and nuclear terrorism prevention purposes by eliminating more HEU.[38] The private Nuclear Threat Initiative has also been trying to stimulate further expansion of this program—for instance, by funding studies by Russian experts to examine the financial costs and technical resources required to implement various options.[39]

Although Russia has shown little interest in extending the Megatons-to-Megawatts program, Washington and Moscow should renew efforts to negotiate a new agreement to convert several hundred more tons of weapons uranium into reactor fuel, even though an expanded program can succeed only with buy-in from the commercial nuclear industry.

MULTILATERAL NUCLEAR ARMS CONTROL AND RISK REDUCTION

The United States and Russia were the first countries to develop nuclear weapons and they have built the largest nuclear arsenals. They were also the first countries to commercialize nuclear power, and still play leading roles in the global nuclear industry. Further, they joined political forces in the 1960s to lead international efforts to enact the NPT. Thus, they clearly have the responsibility and a mutual interest to lead global efforts to reduce nuclear arms, increase prospects for the use of nuclear energy, and strengthen the nonproliferation regime.

If the United States and Russia can achieve deeper nuclear arms reductions through a future bilateral arms control agreement, the question remains: How much lower can they reduce their arsenals before they would need to involve other nuclear-armed states in the arms control process? As one expert has noted, if the United States and Russia decrease their arsenals to a thousand warheads each and "if emerging nuclear weapons states continue to increase their capacity to make and deploy more nuclear weapons, the results in ten years time could be a set of nuclear arms rivalries that will be far more intense and tighter than any experienced since the outset of the Cold War."[40] China, India, and Pakistan, in particular, could have nuclear arsenals that start to rival the size of American and Russian arsenals.

In the coming years, more states may have nuclear weapons as a result of the spread of technologies with weapons-related applications, such as enrichment and reprocessing. This situation would complicate the challenge of promoting political stability and preventing nuclear weapons use. Multilateral arms control offers one way to manage this complex challenge. But states have not yet developed the conditions required for multilateral nuclear arms control. Thus, the United States and Russia need to include as an essential part of their strategic dialogue a discussion of ways to lessen the risks of more nuclear-armed states.

The Task Force believes that multilateral arms control will require years to develop and implement, but that further arms reductions in the near term between Russia and the United States would increase the likelihood of achieving longer-term steps toward assured multilateral commitments to global nuclear arms reductions.

U.S.-China Relations

China is a nuclear-armed rival—but not an enemy—of the United States. Recent U.S. administrations have vacillated about whether to consider China a strategic partner or a competitor. Like Russia, China has taken steps to improve its nuclear capabilities. "Of the five original nuclear weapon states, China alone is believed to be increasing its nuclear arsenal, boosting its numbers by roughly 25 percent since 2005, according to Pentagon estimates."[41] In recent years, China is estimated to have added modern, solid-fueled, three-stage DF-31A ICBMs to its older stockpile of about only two dozen liquid-fueled, silo-based nuclear-armed ballistic missiles capable of reaching the United States.[42] Estimates of the total Chinese nuclear stockpile vary from eighty to almost three hundred warheads.[43] In addition to missile modernization, China has recently deployed the first of a projected new class of ballistic missile submarines, though its operational status remains questionable.[44]

The January 2007 Chinese antisatellite weapon test also raised concern that China may adopt a more aggressive posture, even as China cautiously watches U.S. missile defense programs. Conversely, the United States is carefully assessing Chinese military modernization. As Defense Secretary Robert M. Gates observed, "Beijing's investments in cyberwarfare, antisatellite warfare, antiaircraft and antiship weaponry, submarines, and ballistic missiles could threaten the United States' primary means to project its power and help its allies in the Pacific: bases, air and sea assets, and the networks that support them. This will put a premium on the United States' ability to strike from over the horizon and employ missile defenses and will require shifts from short-range to longer-range systems, such as the next-generation bomber."[45] His statement on missile defenses could be read by Chinese military planners as a U.S. attempt to undermine China's nuclear deterrent based on long-range ballistic missiles. The U.S. intelligence community has recently assessed that "Beijing seeks to modernize China's strategic forces in order to address concerns about the survivability of those systems in the face of foreign, particularly U.S., advances in strategic reconnaissance, precision strike, and missile defenses. . . . China's nuclear capabilities will increase over the next ten years."[46]

In light of these assessments, the Task Force believes that the United States needs to better clarify the intention of its force posture in Asia and missile defense plans, and that China needs to be more transparent about the aims of its military modernization efforts.

Following a midair collision between a Chinese fighter and a U.S. Navy surveillance aircraft over Hainan in early 2001, tensions led to a lengthy hiatus in U.S.-China military-to-military dialogue. Beijing and Washington have renewed this discussion, but it remains at a nascent stage in terms of trust and openness. Not surprisingly, Beijing remains reluctant to open the dialogue to a detailed discussion of sensitive nuclear weapons issues. With a relatively small arsenal and little early-warning capability of impending attack, China has understandably cultivated strategic ambiguity. The most plausible—some would say the only likely—near-term scenario that could bring China and the United States to a nuclear brink would be an attempt to change the status quo in the Taiwan Strait, either by a move toward formal Taiwanese independence or by China seeking to incorporate the island by force.

Concerning its nuclear weapons declaratory policy, China has adopted a no-first-use pledge, which may still allow it to use nuclear weapons first in a self-defense counterattack against a nuclear-armed state or a conflict involving Taiwan. In December 2006, the Chinese government described its "defensive nuclear strategy" in a statement:

> China's nuclear strategy is subject to the state's nuclear policy and military strategy. Its fundamental goal is to deter other countries from using or threatening to use nuclear weapons against China. China remains firmly committed to the policy of no first use of nuclear weapons at any time and under any circumstances. It unconditionally undertakes not to use or threaten to use nuclear weapons against nonnuclear-weapon states or nuclear-weapon-free zones, and stands for the comprehensive prohibition and complete elimination of nuclear weapons. China upholds the principles of counterattack in self-defense and limited development of nuclear weapons, and aims at building a lean and effective nuclear force capable of meeting national security needs.

It endeavors to ensure the security and reliability of its nuclear weapons and maintains a credible nuclear deterrent force.[47]

Economic interdependence provides an incentive to avoid military conflict and nuclear confrontation. Although the United States has expressed concern about the growing trade deficit with China, the economies of the two countries have become increasingly intertwined and interdependent. U.S. consumers have bought massive quantities of cheap Chinese goods, and Beijing has lent huge amounts of money to the United States. Similarly, Taiwan and the mainland are increasingly bound in a reciprocal economic relationship. These economic relationships should reduce the probability of a confrontation between China and Taiwan, and keep the United States and China from approaching the nuclear brink, were such a confrontation to occur. On other nuclear issues, China and the United States have generally supported each other, as they did in the six-party talks to dismantle North Korea's nuclear weapons programs. Here, the supportive Beijing-Washington relationship points toward potentially promising dialogues on larger strategic issues.

China is embedded in other complicated nuclear-related relationships. In Northeast Asia, China has worked with the United States through the six party talks—also including Japan, Russia, and South Korea—to try to dismantle North Korea's nuclear weapons programs. Chinese security analysts have repeatedly expressed concerns about Japan's latent nuclear weapons capability and that a reunified Korea could become another nuclear threat, especially if South Korea inherits North Korea's nuclear weapons. In South Asia, Beijing has a long-standing friendship with Pakistan, a state China has helped acquire civilian—and most likely military—nuclear capabilities. This friendship is balanced against Beijing's rivalry with New Delhi as these two Asian giants emerge as economic powerhouses. Although China and India have largely reconciled the dispute that led to their 1962 border war, each has partially paced its strategic weapons program on the other's capabilities. Finally, China has to take into account Russia's nuclear weapons when thinking about force posture in military planning.

An important point of departure in any U.S.-China strategic dialogue is a discussion of China's perceptions of its security environment. Similarly, the United States needs to clearly articulate its interests. However, because of the large asymmetry between the U.S. and Chinese nuclear arsenals, the Task Force finds that negotiating a formal arms control agreement with China is not a useful or realistic objective for the foreseeable future.

A significant issue for China is whether the United States is willing to accept mutual vulnerability as the basis of strategic relations between the two states. The United States accepts mutual vulnerability between the United States and Russia as a strategic fact and thus deals with threats from Russia through deterrence. At the same time, the United States seeks to prevent the emergence of actual or latent nuclear-armed states such as Iran and North Korea. The United States has not, thus far, decided whether China is a small Russia to be deterred or a large North Korea to be defended against. The Task Force concludes that mutual vulnerability with China—like mutual vulnerability with Russia—is not a policy choice to be embraced or rejected, but rather a strategic fact to be managed with priority on strategic stability.

Given this conclusion, the United States has a clear interest in increased dialogue with China on a range of strategic issues, including U.S. ballistic missile defenses aimed against North Korea. Such a dialogue could help temper the risk of increased Chinese nuclear modernization to counter U.S. ballistic missile defenses without any major improvement in the U.S. ability to limit damage from China. The transparency and confidence-building measures the United States suggested to Russia in 2007 in connection with European ballistic missile defense deployment should be reviewed for applicability to China. Transparency and confidence-building measures associated with ballistic missile defense should play a major role in a U.S.-China strategic dialogue.

Both China and the United States have recently demonstrated antisatellite capabilities. Kinetic antisatellite weapons can destroy both civilian and military satellites with projectiles fired from land, air, or space-based launching systems. Because the United States relies far more on satellites for commercial and military activities, it is far more vulnerable to antisatellite weapons than China is.[48] However, the United States has refused to discuss space weapons with China and has insisted on complete freedom of action in space. The Task Force believes that the United States has a clear interest in beginning discussions with China on space weapons, including proposals to ban tests of kinetic antisatellite weapons. The United States and China, along with Russia, should take the lead in implementing a trilateral test ban, which could form the basis for expansion to a global ban.

Preventing Proliferation

Increasing global access to weapons-usable nuclear materials, and the technologies used to make them, has substantially challenged the United States in its mission of preventing nuclear weapons acquisition and use. Further proliferation will likely raise the risks of strategic miscalculation and increase the probability of nuclear use, particularly if it happens quickly and involves actors that oppose the mainstream international order. Presently, seven states—China, France, India, Pakistan, Russia, the United Kingdom, and the United States—have demonstrated the capability to make nuclear weapons; Israel is widely believed to have the capability but has not explicitly acknowledged this status as a matter of policy; and though North Korea detonated a low-yield nuclear device in October 2006, it may not yet have the ability to deploy nuclear weapons.

Proliferation could increase in the coming decades. About half a dozen nonnuclear weapon states, including Argentina, Brazil, Iran, Japan, and South Africa, either have or have had enrichment or reprocessing facilities that could provide weapons-usable uranium or plutonium. Dozens of other states may acquire these capabilities, depending on the demand for civilian nuclear power and the ability of the international community to limit the spread of national enrichment and reprocessing facilities. A growth in the number of states acquiring nuclear weapons or the ability to quickly make such weapons could have deeply adverse effects on U.S. national security and the security of American allies.

In addition, the risk of global terrorism may increase with further nuclear weapons proliferation. Terrorists seeking nuclear weapons could look to state facilities to acquire weapons-usable fissile material to make improvised nuclear explosives or to acquire intact nuclear weapons. Weapons-usable fissile materials—highly enriched uranium and plutonium—do not exist in nature. To make these materials, certain states have invested significant financial and industrial resources in two technologies: enrichment and reprocessing. Enrichment increases the concentration of the fissile isotope of uranium. At low enrichments, the uranium can be used only to fuel nuclear reactors. At higher enrichment, the uranium becomes weapons-usable.[49] What is particularly problematic in terms of proliferation prevention is that the same technology used to produce low-enriched uranium (LEU) can also be used to make HEU for weapon purposes. Even a pilot-scale enrichment plant like the one Iran has built can produce at least enough HEU for one bomb per year.[50]

As for reprocessing, to produce enough plutonium for at least one bomb annually, a state would need at least a medium-sized nuclear reactor and a reprocessing plant to separate the plutonium from spent nuclear fuel. As with enrichment, reprocessing is a dual-use technology. It makes either nuclear fuel for reactors or fissile material for nuclear weapons.

Terrorists now and for the foreseeable future do not have the wherewithal to enrich their own uranium or produce their own plutonium. Instead, they would have to target state stockpiles of these materials. To acquire nuclear weapons, a terrorist group could try to buy or steal existing weapons or weapons-usable fissile material, or convince or coerce a government custodian to hand over these assets.

The overarching strategy to prevent terrorists and more states from acquiring nuclear weapons involves strengthening the nonproliferation regime, stopping the production of fissile material for weapons purposes, controlling the spread of enrichment and reprocessing technologies, and securing and reducing, as much as possible, nuclear weapons and weapons-usable materials. This chapter presents analysis and findings on all of these efforts, except for securing and reducing weapons and materials, a subject addressed in the next chapter. To further reduce the risk of nuclear terrorism, it is also important to interdict these weapons and materials if they fall into terrorist hands and to take broad counterterrorism measures, but such strategies are beyond the scope of this report.

ENSURING A SUCCESSFUL 2010 NONPROLIFERATION TREATY REVIEW CONFERENCE

In the 1960s, the United States led global efforts to create the nuclear Nonproliferation Treaty. In its preamble, the NPT, which entered into force in 1970, underscores "the devastation that would be visited upon all mankind by a nuclear war and the consequent need to make every effort to avert the danger of such a war . . . [and] that the proliferation of nuclear weapons would seriously enhance the danger of nuclear war." The NPT has three main objectives: to keep as many states as possible from becoming nuclear-armed, to contribute to the spread of peaceful nuclear technology, and to commit nuclear and nonnuclear weapon states "to pursue negotiations in good faith on effective measures relating to cessation of the nuclear arms race at an early date and to nuclear disarmament, and a Treaty on general and complete disarmament under strict and effective international control." As an incentive for nonnuclear weapon states to not acquire nuclear weapons, the NPT provides for access to peaceful nuclear technologies contingent on these states not seeking to develop nuclear weaponry and maintaining safeguards on their civilian nuclear programs.

Every five years, parties to the NPT convene to review the treaty's vitality. In 1995, the United States and other nuclear weapon states helped win the indefinite extension of the treaty by reaffirming their "good faith" commitment to pursue disarmament and stating that they would try to complete the Comprehensive Test Ban Treaty (CTBT) negotiations no later than 1996. At the 2000 NPT Review Conference, the United States and other nuclear weapon states once again affirmed their commitment to work in good faith toward nuclear disarmament and said that they sought to "without delay and without conditions . . . achieve the early entry into force of the Comprehensive Nuclear Test Ban Treaty." But the Senate voted against advice and consent of the CTBT in 1999, and the Bush administration decided not to pursue ratification.

At the 2000 conference, the United States and other NPT member states, especially the nonnuclear weapon states, supported a set of proposals known as the thirteen steps:

− achieving the CTBT's entry into force;
− maintaining the moratorium on nuclear testing;
− negotiating a production ban on fissile material for weapons purposes within five years in the Conference on Disarmament;
− establishing a committee in the Conference on Disarmament to address nuclear disarmament;
− applying the principle of irreversibility to nuclear arms reductions;

- committing the nuclear weapon states to accomplishing the total elimination of their nuclear arsenals;

- calling on the United States and Russia to implement START II, conclude START III, and preserve the Anti-Ballistic Missile (ABM) Treaty;

- implementing the Trilateral Initiative among the United States, Russia, and the IAEA;

- calling on the nuclear weapon states to promote international security, in part through further nuclear arms reductions and increased transparency about their nuclear weapons programs;

- placing excess fissile material slated for weapons under monitoring by the IAEA;

- reaffirming general and complete disarmament under effective international control;

- issuing regular reports by the nuclear weapon states on the implementation of nuclear disarmament; and

- developing verification capabilities to assure compliance with disarmament agreements.

None of these steps has been fully carried out, though significant progress has been made on some of them. With respect to nuclear arms control, the United States and Russia did not implement START II and III, but instead formed the 2002 Treaty of Moscow, a less constraining and less formal treaty, as discussed earlier in this report. The United States left the ABM Treaty to develop and deploy a national missile defense system, but continued to reduce the number of nuclear warheads deployed on strategic delivery systems and to dismantle retired warheads. Since the thirteen steps were issued, the United States has declared additional fissile material as not necessary for weapons purposes. Although the United States and Russia did begin to create a verification system for weapon origin and other excess fissile material under the Trilateral Initiative with the IAEA, the initiative stalled because the two countries were not convinced it would improve the nonproliferation system. The United States should lead by example on steps that specifically call for making further nuclear arms reductions, taking irreversible actions on nuclear warhead dismantlement, and increasing the transparency of nuclear weapons posture and policy.

Before the 2005 conference, the treaty was challenged by developments in Iran and North Korea and by the inability of other NPT members, especially the nuclear weapon states, to adopt stiff measures to enforce compliance or punish noncompliance. Iran has stated that it is developing a peaceful nuclear program, but has acquired as part of that program the means to enrich uranium and is obtaining a type of reactor optimally suited for weapons-grade plutonium production. Some of Iran's activities involving its nuclear program have violated its safeguards agreement under the NPT, for which it has been sanctioned by the UN Security Council. The Iranian nuclear program could also stimulate further proliferation in the Middle East as neighboring states hedge against Iran's growing nuclear capability. In 2003, North Korea became the first signatory state to leave the treaty. It has since proceeded to separate more plutonium for weapons and in 2006 tested a nuclear device. The Obama administration has just over a year to prepare for the 2010 NPT Review Conference. The Task Force urges the new administration to move quickly in deciding on its positions, mustering the diplomatic efforts required to avoid failure at the conference, and leading efforts to strengthen the nonproliferation regime. A successful conference would require that the United States treat it not as a perfunctory international meeting, but instead as an opportunity to exert U.S. leadership and bring together nuclear and nonnuclear weapon states to think about their interests and the global changes needed to strengthen international security. The parties to the conference have a strong interest in reexamining and reaffirming the rights and responsibilities of both nuclear and nonnuclear weapon states.

In regard to the responsibility of nuclear weapon states to pursue disarmament in good faith, the United States needs to ensure that concerns about its disarmament record do not preclude its ability to advance an appropriate agenda during the conference. The United States has often found itself on the defensive, accused of not doing enough to reduce nuclear arms. Recognizing that the political conditions that will lead to abolition are rather daunting, the United States can still lead on this objective by having serious discussions about conditions for achieving further nuclear arms reductions. It can put the onus on itself and all countries interested in disarmament to provide insights about necessary political, security, and technical preconditions. The United States has a strong interest in explaining the significant steps it has already taken toward nuclear disarmament and in reaffirming its commitment to determining what type of security environment could ensure that nuclear weapons are never used.

The nonproliferation regime serves the interests of the nonnuclear weapon states by helping ensure that their neighbors, rivals, and enemies do not acquire nuclear weapons. These states need to first acknowledge the principle that they have responsibilities for and a significant national security interest in maintaining the nonproliferation regime and then, with the nuclear weapon states, properly interpret the rights and responsibilities. Article IV of the NPT, which speaks of an inalienable right to civilian nuclear technologies, is subject to two obligations. First, it is contingent on a nonnuclear weapon state adhering to Article II stipulations "not to manufacture or otherwise acquire nuclear weapons or other nuclear explosive devices; and not to seek or receive any assistance in the manufacture of nuclear weapons or other nuclear explosive devices." Second, this right is contingent on maintaining safeguards on nuclear programs "in accordance with the Statute of the International Atomic Energy Agency and the Agency's safeguards system." Any state found in noncompliance with its safeguards agreement is subject to action from the UN Security Council. Third, all states, including nonnuclear weapon states, share the Article VI obligation to pursue nuclear disarmament.

The Task Force concludes that the United States has an interest in leading states at the 2010 NPT Review Conference to shore up the Article IV provision for access to peaceful nuclear technologies. States would reaffirm that this access depends on maintaining rigorous safeguards and on confidence that no action to acquire nuclear explosive devices has been taken. By making this affirmation, the nonnuclear weapon states will also underscore their commitment to pursuing nuclear disarmament.

To make such a reaffirmation even more meaningful, more rigorous safeguards can be placed on all states' civilian nuclear programs. In particular, the IAEA has developed the Additional Protocol to states' comprehensive safeguards agreements.[51] Under the Additional Protocol, inspectors are required to assess whether a state has any undeclared nuclear facilities or materials. One of the Bush administration's last acts was to enter into force the U.S. ratification of the Additional Protocol, which it did on January 9, 2009. Although about ninety states have signed the Additional Protocol, the board of governors has yet to make it a mandatory requirement on states; some major developing nations, such as Brazil and Egypt, view it as an additional and unnecessary burden. Encouragingly, the states of Central Asia recently enacted a nuclear weapon–free zone that legally requires them to apply the Additional Protocol.

The Task Force believes that the Additional Protocol should become mandatory for any state desiring access to commercial nuclear power, and that this issue deserves attention at the 2010 NPT Review Conference. But the United States may not be able to win enough support for this move in time for the review conference because leading developing states have already resisted a similar proposal. The Additional Protocol is also not a miracle cure for safeguards problems. A state subject to it could still develop a clandestine nuclear weapons program, though hiding such activities would be more difficult. In addition, to allow the IAEA to cut costs, states that have undergone the inspection process and have a good track record of compliance with safeguards are subject to fewer inspections. However, to help deter any deception, even an upstanding state should continue to be subject to periodic inspections.

The Task Force supports ensuring that the IAEA's safeguards department has adequate financial resources to carry out this important job by making each state's contribution to the safeguards budget directly proportional to its use of nuclear power and the amount of its nuclear materials subject to safeguards.[52] Further, the Task Force urges the United States to initiate discussions between and research by both nuclear and nonnuclear weapon states about improving safeguards beyond the Additional Protocol. Such improvements should include more research and development on wide-area monitoring for the presence of clandestine enrichment and reprocessing plants, and the application of near-real-time monitoring of nuclear facilities and materials.

Also in need of attention is the risk that a state can withdraw from the treaty, keep nuclear technologies and materials acquired as a member, and use these capabilities to make nuclear weapons. Specifically, Article X allows a state to withdraw from the treaty after giving three months' notice, "if it decides that extraordinary events, related to the subject matter of this Treaty, have jeopardized the supreme interests of its country." To prevent use of nuclear technologies and materials in weapons programs, because the NPT is by design effectively impossible to amend, challenges posed by states like North Korea, which withdrew from the treaty, must be dealt with by new mechanisms that are outside the treaty but consistent with it.

Many nonnuclear weapon states do not want to be burdened with additional rules imposed on them. But the NPT member states and the nonproliferation system as a whole benefit when the rules are tightened and clarified. Thus, the member states have an interest in carefully assessing how to update the rules in light of experience and technological developments, in general, and to clarify the process of withdrawal, in particular. The UN Security Council has the responsibility to work with these states in enforcing these rules.

Two categories of states could express interest in exercising the withdrawal clause: those in compliance and those not in compliance with their safeguards commitments. For both, the UN Security Council has an interest in assessing the circumstances of withdrawal and determining whether the state can be convinced to remain inside the treaty. For those states not in compliance when expressing interest in withdrawal, the Security Council has a clear interest in calling for special inspections to determine whether a clandestine weapons program exists. The Security Council and the NPT Review Conference attendees could consider an even more controversial "return to sender" proposal. They could require that nuclear materials and technologies acquired while the withdrawing state was noncompliant be returned to the countries of origin. Although the Security Council would find it difficult to achieve, this action lies clearly in the interests of international security.

The United States could also submit a finding at the NPT Review Conference that the three-month withdrawal period stipulated by Article X does not allow states enough time to resolve problems that led to the "extraordinary events" provoking withdrawal, as demonstrated in the recent past. The finding could propose, instead, an agreement that would lengthen this withdrawal period to one year.

Although states have the sovereign right to invoke the supreme national interest clause to exit the NPT or other arms control treaties, the United States has an interest in leading states at the forthcoming conference to correct weaknesses in the Article X withdrawal clause. The United States should propose that any withdrawing state return nuclear technologies and materials acquired while in noncompliance to countries of origin and that the UN Security Council pass a resolution to establish a special inspections team to monitor materials before they are returned to the states of origin. The team would ensure that withdrawing states did not misuse technologies and materials acquired to produce nuclear weapons. Enforcing these proposed corrections to the Article X withdrawal clause would be difficult but worthwhile.

COMPREHENSIVE TEST BAN TREATY

The Comprehensive Test Ban Treaty, a long-standing issue on the nuclear arms control agenda, would ban all nuclear test explosions worldwide if and when it enters into force. For this to happen, all forty-four of the Annex 2 states, which have significant nuclear capabilities, must ratify the treaty—a challenging prospect.[53] Though thirty-five of these states have completed ratification (as of October 2008), several important nations remain outside the fold. China and the United States have signed the treaty but not ratified it. India, North Korea, and Pakistan, who have done neither, have all tested nuclear weapons since 1998. None of the de jure nuclear weapon states has conducted a nuclear weapons test since 1996. India and Pakistan, however, which have conducted relatively few tests, would likely welcome the opportunity to renew testing if the de facto moratorium were lifted and the international norm against testing weakened or collapsed.

The treaty offers distinct technical and political benefits. Of the technical advantages, the CTBT would make it harder for a nuclear-armed state to develop new advanced nuclear weapons, such as thermonuclear warheads or miniaturized weapons. But it would not prevent all modernization or refurbishment of existing nuclear arsenals. Nuclear-armed states maintain the vitality of these arsenals using many tools short of nuclear testing. The CTBT would also have little or no effect in halting the development of first-generation uranium-based nuclear weapons, such as the atomic bomb detonated on Hiroshima. Entry into force would provide the technical benefit of on-site inspections, especially in the event of a suspected nuclear test.

Arguably, the greatest near-term advantage of entry into force is that India and Pakistan would not resume nuclear testing and thereby expand their arsenals with thermonuclear weapons, which are more lethal than the devices currently in their respective stockpiles. Independent experts have expressed considerable doubt that the rounds of South Asian nuclear tests in May 1998 demonstrated thermonuclear capabilities. In fact, some Indian and Pakistani politicians and nuclear scientists have expressed interest in additional nuclear tests. New Delhi and Islamabad have therefore resisted even signing the treaty. Ratification by China and the United States, however, will apply political pressure on India and Pakistan to do the same, though there is no guarantee that they would do so.

Another benefit would be to raise the cost of nuclear weapons acquisition for Tehran. If Iranian leaders decided to build nuclear weapons, they could at some point seek to test them—to gain prestige, to signal in a crisis, or to build the technical confidence required to produce a credible arsenal. Testing under a CTBT would be a stark violation of a new international treaty endorsed by the entire world and would risk lost prestige, isolation, and sanctions, whereas testing in a world where the United States (and Israel) continued to block a CTBT would leave ready excuses for states to look the other way.

With regard to long-term technical benefits, the CTBT would place an additional hurdle in the way of states seeking nuclear weapons. Following the rules of Article X, a government interested in nuclear weapons would have to either develop a covert program or withdraw from the NPT. The CTBT's entry into force would also provide an extra degree of technical constraint. Proliferators would no longer be certain that their nuclear weapons work, unless they are willing to rely on untested first-generation weapons.

The CTBT's entry into force could shore up support among U.S. allies and other nonnuclear weapon states to further strengthen the nonproliferation regime. Although the CTBT itself would not stop a determined proliferator, its conclusion and U.S. support for it were clearly linked to the indefinite extension of the NPT. Thus, U.S. ratification has become, in the eyes of many states, a litmus test for U.S. leadership in the overall global effort to prevent the use and spread of nuclear weapons. Although it would not ensure entry into force, U.S. ratification would put Washington in a position to pressure holdout states to ratify the treaty. Furthermore, U.S. ratification would promote international norm building that would stigmatize states that conduct nuclear testing; it would increase the likelihood that states that violate this norm would be punished.

The entry into force of the CTBT would also deter a state from conducting tests as a form of blackmail, intimidation, or political posturing. For example, the primary purpose of the North Korean test may have been to blackmail China, the United States, Japan, and South Korea for more aid. The Indian tests in May 1998 are also widely believed to have been a means to consolidate support for the nationalist Bharatiya Janata

Party, which had risen to power just a few months before the tests and had made testing part of its political campaign platform.

Given the daunting, if not impossible, task of delinking the CTBT from the nonproliferation regime, what options are in U.S. interests? For one, the United States could continue its testing moratorium without ratification. This option would obviously not bring the CTBT into force and would not garner the political and technical benefits discussed.

Because nuclear tests would provide confidence that replacement warheads are in working order, the United States has the option under international law—because it has not yet ratified the treaty—of doing a round of proof tests. Congress, however, would almost certainly refuse to permit this. Furthermore, there has been no support for it within the weapons design community. Proponents of these warheads, therefore, support their development without nuclear testing. Even if the United States did ratify the treaty, it could withdraw under the extraordinary events clause if Washington had reason to suspect that its nuclear deterrent was at risk because enough warheads in the arsenal were not safe or reliable. A return-to-testing option, however, carries huge political risks. The United States would open the door for China, India, Pakistan, and Russia to also conduct tests, and would risk losing international support on improving the nonproliferation regime.

President Obama has called for the United States to ratify the treaty. The CTBT's ratification depends strongly on the prevailing political climate. In October 2008, Secretary of Defense Gates expressed support for ratification, as long as concerns about verification can be addressed, and offered his view that a credible deterrent cannot be maintained without eventually resorting to testing or pursuing a nuclear weapons complex modernization program. He advocated the latter option and specifically proposed building replacement warheads.[54] Further, an additional decade's experience with stockpile stewardship (discussed in the next chapter) and with verification may mitigate the substantive concerns of treaty opponents. Conversely, few senators pay close attention to arms control issues and thus would require extensive briefings about the significance, provisions, and verification measures of the CTBT.

CTBT critics are concerned that a state could muffle a test in an underground cavity, known as decoupling, or cheat the system some other way. A July 2002 National Academy of Sciences panel report concluded that "verification capabilities for the treaty are better than generally supposed, U.S. adversaries could not significantly advance their nuclear weapons capabilities through tests below the threshold of detection, and the United States has the technical capabilities to maintain confidence in the safety and reliability of its existing weapons stockpile without periodic nuclear tests."[55] Notably, the existing monitoring system detected the low-yield North Korean test in October 2006. Looking forward, the CTBT Preparatory Committee commissioned a project in March 2008 to scientifically evaluate the "readiness and capability" of the CTBT verification regime.[56] In the meantime, the Obama administration should secure a separate agreement with Russia to permit on-site monitoring to ensure that the decoupled tests banned by the CTBT are not being conducted.

There are also concerns about protecting the U.S. nuclear deterrent under the CTBT. Before the 1999 vote, the Clinton administration proposed six safeguards.[57] The administration, in its review, and the Senate, during its consideration of advice and consent, may need to strengthen or modify some of these safeguards and even include additional ones. The Task Force considers it important that the United States retain the capability, if necessary, to improve the reliability of existing warheads, to incorporate modern safety and security features, and to exercise occasionally the design skills of weapon scientists. The Task Force also favors having the executive branch provide a detailed report to the Senate at least every four years—to ensure that an assessment occurs during each presidential term—on whether the CTBT continues to meet U.S. security interests.

If the United States is to ratify the CTBT, it would be useful to be at or near ratification by the 2010 Review Conference to gain related, substantive political benefits. Because thorough Senate consideration will be important, both technically and politically, this suggested ratification timing indicates that Senate hearings need to begin by late 2009.

PRODUCTION OF FISSILE MATERIAL FOR WEAPONS PURPOSES

Without fissile material, a state cannot make nuclear weapons. Without access to this material manufactured by states, a nuclear terrorist group cannot make an improvised nuclear device. Consequently, to prevent both state proliferation and nuclear terrorism, controlling fissile material production is important. This section focuses on fissile material produced by states to develop weapons. The following section examines fissile material in nonweapons applications that can still power nuclear explosive devices.

Significant global progress has already been made in halting the production of fissile material for weapons purposes. France, Russia, the United Kingdom, and the United States—four of the five de jure nuclear weapon states—have officially declared the end of their fissile material production. Russia, the United Kingdom, and the United States have also declared that their reserves of HEU and plutonium exceed their defense needs by many tons, and have been working transparently to make much of this material unusable for weapons purposes.

The states holding out on declaring an end to fissile material production for weapons purposes are China, India, Israel, North Korea, and Pakistan. The opacity of Israel's nuclear weapons programs has made it difficult to determine whether Israel is producing fissile material. Israel is believed, however, to have produced fissile material for weapons at its Dimona nuclear facility, which is nearing the end of its functionality. The pending closure of this facility could present an opportunity for Israel to invite the IAEA to certify Dimona's decommissioning and to refrain from building a new fissile material production facility. Thus, without making a formal announcement about any past fissile material production, by decommissioning Dimona and refraining from building a similar replacement reactor, Israel could signal to other states in the region its interest in supporting a fissile material cutoff.[58]

The Task Force supports the Obama administration's working closely with partners to keep North Korea to its commitment to verifiably dismantle all its nuclear weapons programs. North Korea had halted plutonium production at Yongbyon as a result of the six-party talks, but it is unclear whether it has produced or is producing highly enriched uranium. Pyongyang recently tried to condition its commitment to end fissile material production and dismantlement of its nuclear weapons programs on having access to South Korea to verify the absence of U.S. nuclear weapons there. However, the United States removed all of its nuclear weapons on the Korean Peninsula in the early 1990s, under the orders of then president George H.W. Bush. Moreover, the United States has reaffirmed repeatedly this stand-down of its forces. In addition, North Korean leaders know that the United States can strike North Korea with nuclear weapons using long-range bomb-ers such as the B2 and long-range ballistic missiles such as Minuteman III or Trident missiles. Changes in U.S. nuclear posture would likely have little or no direct influence on North Korea's meeting its obliga-tion to stop fissile material production and verifiably dismantle its nuclear weapons programs.

In contrast, U.S. actions on nuclear posture and missile defense have a direct bearing on China's decisions on its nuclear force structure and thus its fissile material production. China is a particularly pivotal state in this respect because of its quadrangular relationship with India, Paki-stan, and the United States. While U.S.-China nuclear relations are dis-cussed in more depth in the previous chapter, the salient points here are that China has a relatively small nuclear arsenal, especially inter-continental ballistic missiles, compared to the United States; Chinese military planners have expressed concern about U.S. missile defense capabilities against China's relatively small (for now) long-range mis-sile force; and China, depending on the evolution of strategic relations with the United States, may want to increase the size of its nuclear arse-nal in the coming decades. Faced with this security environment with respect to the United States, it is understandable that China would not want to make any formal declaration about fissile material production. The U.S. Defense Intelligence Agency recently determined that "China likely has produced enough weapons-grade fissile material to meet its needs for the immediate future."[59]

China's fissile material status has a direct effect on India. Although the two countries have dramatically improved relations with each other since their 1962 border war, they continue to be rivals. Fur-thermore, Indian military planners have partly linked India's nuclear deterrent to China's. If China continues to build up its nuclear forces—though this may be in response to the United States—India will likely feel compelled to follow suit. This may lead, in turn, to Pakistan increasing its production of fissile material, given the India-Pakistan nuclear arms race.

China has linked the proposed Fissile Material Cutoff Treaty (FMCT), which the United States has supported, to the draft treaty Prevention of an Arms Race in Outer Space, which the United States has opposed. This impasse has contributed to the complicated set of political factors that have deadlocked FMCT negotiations in the UN Conference on Disarmament, a multilateral arms control forum based in Geneva that requires consensus to even begin negotiations. Because the mechanism of the Conference on Disarmament has led to a stalemate on discussion of an FMCT, the United States would obtain better traction by initiating parallel discussions with China, India, Pakistan, and other nuclear-armed states.

Although the United States has advocated for a ban on fissile material production, the Bush administration concluded that effective verification measures for such a treaty were not feasible. The May 2006 draft FMCT contains no verification provisions, an omission that has drawn criticism from international nonproliferation advocates.

The Task Force recognizes that although an FMCT faces daunting political and technical hurdles, the United States has an interest in efforts to ban the production of fissile material for weapons purposes. Although an FMCT is not as meaningful as reductions in the stockpiles of fissile material, it is an important step toward that objective, especially for states that are continuing their production of fissile material for weapons purposes. The United States should renew technical studies to assess the feasibility of an effectively verifiable FMCT. The issue of verification, however, is of less concern than the opposition of China, India, and Pakistan to an FMCT. The Task Force acknowledges that the impediments to bringing about an FMCT will not be resolved by the 2010 NPT Review Conference, but it supports the United States taking the lead in calling for a moratorium on fissile material production before the conference. Such a call alone will not convince China, India, and Pakistan to support an FMCT, but it could help rally many states to support further strengthening the nonproliferation regime—for instance, by shoring up Article IV commitments.

FISSILE MATERIAL IN NONWEAPONS APPLICATIONS

The proposed FMCT applies only to fissile material produced for weapons purposes. But nonweapons HEU—for instance, the approximately fifty metric tons of HEU used in the civilian sector—could still pose security problems.[60] The United States and Russia have had programs since the late 1970s to phase out the use of HEU in civilian research reactors. In 2004, the Bush administration reenergized these programs and placed them under the umbrella Global Threat Reduction Initiative

(GTRI). GTRI doubled the pace of HEU removal operations compared to the previous program. But more than half of the identified material remains to be secured and removed. In early 2009, the GTRI developed an action plan for accomplishing its remaining mission within the next four years, President Obama's target time frame for securing loose nuclear material. In addition, the GTRI has sped up the conversion of HEU-fueled research reactors to use low-enriched uranium fuels and has supported additional research into developing new high density LEU fuels to convert reactors that cannot use existing LEU fuels.[61] The United States has converted most of its HEU-fueled reactors.

The Task Force believes the United States has a strong interest in expanding and devoting enough financial and human resources to the Global Threat Reduction Initiative to cover more HEU reactors, convert the remaining HEU reactors as quickly as technically feasible, and complete HEU security and removal operations by the end of 2012.

Despite this progress, significant impediments remain. Russia continues to use HEU in research reactors (none of which are slated to be converted to LEU), critical assemblies (a type of test reactor), and ice-breakers (which, independent studies indicate, can be converted to use LEU fuel).[62] Though there are some technical challenges to conversion, the main obstacles are political. To facilitate conversion or decommissioning, Russia should be offered incentives, such as scientific cooperation in cutting-edge computer simulations to substitute for the critical assemblies and the consolidation of as many HEU facilities as possible into a few research centers with enhanced security features.

Canada, Belgium, the Netherlands, and South Africa also continue to use HEU in producing medical isotopes, on which millions across the globe rely. Converting to LEU production targets is technically feasible.[63] The real pushback comes from manufacturers, who are concerned about the costs of conversion and the added waste from LEU target processing. U.S. and international efforts should continue to promote and fund more research on the use of nonweapons-usable uranium in civilian applications such as medical and commercial isotope production, and the United States should work with these producers to determine a desirable yet cost-effective package of incentives to facilitate isotope production conversion to low-enriched uranium.

Even if these commercial concerns were resolved, the United States would continue to face political resistance from South Africa on phasing out its HEU stockpile. South Africa has an estimated stockpile of six ıundred kilograms of HEU—enough to make at least a dozen nuclear bombs—which it verifiably dismantled by the early 1990s. As the only state that has completely dismantled a nuclear weapons program, South Africa perceives itself as a leading nation in championing nuclear disarmament. It has also stood up for the rights of developing countries to use peaceful nuclear technologies, including isotope production for commercial purposes. South Africa has therefore resisted calls from the United States to give up its HEU stockpile. It believes that the United States and the other nuclear-armed states need to first do more to reduce their own HEU stockpiles and pursue nuclear disarmament. But Pretoria's ability to secure its HEU was put in question when its Pelindaba facility suffered a (fortunately unsuccessful) breach of security in November 2007. Although South Africa has received security assistance from the IAEA, the United States should work with South Africa to determine whether additional security measures are needed to guard South African HEU in the context of a larger dialogue to determine whether a global ban on civilian HEU is feasible.

Just as it does not apply to the civilian use of highly enriched uranium, the FMCT does not apply to the civilian use of reactor-grade plutonium, which can also be used in nuclear explosives. International Atomic Energy Agency safeguards on facilities that enrich uranium and reprocess spent nuclear fuel to extract plutonium provide some assurances that these materials are not diverted into weapons programs. Some of these facilities—such as Tokai-mura in Japan and Sellafield in the United Kingdom, which handle several tons of plutonium annually—have "significant quantities" of fissile material that are unaccounted for, because this material has most likely caked on the pipes and walls of these facilities. (Eight kilograms of plutonium, considered a significant quantity by the IAEA, provides enough material for at least one bomb.) The inevitable difficulty in accounting for all of this material could mask the diversion of small quantities to weapons production.

THE EXPANSION OF NUCLEAR POWER AND ENRICHMENT AND REPROCESSING FACILITIES

Although U.S. nuclear weapons policy does not have a direct link to countries interested in commercial nuclear power, the potential for a major expansion of nuclear energy worldwide has drawn the attention of the Task Force. Concerns about energy security and the risks of global warming have revived interest in commercial nuclear power around the world. At the same time, increases in electricity demand are projected for developing economies in Asia, Africa, and Latin America. Thus, many experts are projecting a possible growth of nuclear power reactors in these regions from fewer than twenty reactors today to more than three hundred reactors by the middle of the century (excluding Japan, South Korea, and Taiwan).[64] Until now, however, no country except India has diverted fissile material from its civilian nuclear power facilities for the production of nuclear weapons.

The challenge is to continue strengthening the separation between nuclear weapons and nuclear power globally. This entails a global effort to ensure that the nuclear power fuel cycle is not used as a source of weapons-usable fissile material. The greatest proliferation risk comes from two elements of the fuel cycle: enrichment of natural uranium to produce nuclear fuel, and reprocessing of the spent reactor fuel to separate plutonium.

Presently, relatively few countries enrich uranium for commercial purposes. The main commercial enrichment facilities are located in France, Germany, the Netherlands, Russia, the United Kingdom, and the United States. All but the U.S. facility, operated by the United States Enrichment Corporation, are fully or partially owned by governments. Brazil, China, and Japan have smaller enrichment facilities, and Argentina, Canada, and South Africa have recently expressed interest—in response to the potential for increased demand for nuclear fuel in the future—in operating commercial enrichment facilities. Other states could join their ranks as well. Given the increased interest in expanding uranium enrichment to new states, the United States has an interest in working with partner states to establish global rules on uranium enrichment to reduce the proliferation risks. Extensive state ownership of uranium enrichment plants gives the governments in question considerable leverage in controlling the future direction of this industry; for instance, governments could make future licensing of these plants contingent on multilateral ownership and control.

To head off the further spread of enrichment facilities, several fuel cycle assurances have been proposed.[65] The core concept is to offer multiple tiers of fuel availability. The existing nuclear fuel market would comprise the first tier. A second tier could consist of a virtual fuel bank of enrichment bonds that would offer insurance coverage and a political commitment by suppliers' governments to ensure fuel supplies as long as recipient states maintain adequate safeguards on their nuclear programs. A third tier could consist of an actual bank of enriched uranium fuel in case the other tiers fail.[66] Most of the proposals would favor multinational ownership of facilities but would restrict access to the actual enrichment or reprocessing technologies by employing "black box" techniques. Thus, countries buying into the facilities would have guaranteed access to the fuel produced, but need not, as a consequence, be apprised of methods of replicating the technologies in overt or covert national facilities. Personnel security programs would be required to help protect this knowledge from unauthorized access.

Despite fuel service proposals, some countries may decide to pursue fuel-making for a variety of reasons: national pride and prestige, the belief that near-term capital expenditure on fuel cycle facilities will pay off in the long term, the view that an indigenous fuel cycle enhances energy security, a defense (by nonaligned movement countries) of the inalienable right under Article IV of the NPT to pursue peaceful nuclear activities, and a hedge against real and perceived security threats by maintaining the latent capacity to make fissile material for bombs. Iran exemplifies all of these factors. Brazil has expressed considerable pride in its enrichment accomplishments and confidence that this investment will eventually pay off, despite the uncertainty of its commercial viability. Nonetheless, fuel service proposals are worth pursuing because several countries—especially those that will acquire only a few reactors—will likely find the economic incentives of refraining from fuel-making attractive.

States can take further steps to prevent the spread of nationally controlled enrichment and reprocessing facilities. The Task Force favors a freeze on all new national enrichment facilities—that is, those under the control or ownership of a single government—and supports governments using their authority to license facilities to implement this freeze. Multinational ownership already exerts control over many of the existing major enrichment plants. Although international control of enrichment and reprocessing is not foolproof, the resultant transparency of these activities is a hedge against their diversion into the production of fissile material for weapons purposes. This depends, of course, on the restriction of access to the technologies and the implementation of enhanced personnel security checks to prevent insiders from transferring the technologies to unauthorized users. The United States also has an interest in working with other uranium enrichment suppliers, in consultation with the IAEA, to provide enriched uranium at a cost that would eliminate the perceived profits of enrichment, but the Task Force is notably not favoring subsidized enrichment. It notes that presently and for the foreseeable future, reprocessing does not make economic sense compared to enrichment.[67] Another mechanism to stem the proliferation threat that additional national enrichment or reprocessing facilities pose is to include an incentive in bilateral nuclear cooperation agreements. That is, fuel suppliers would offer multiple-tiered fuel guarantees in exchange for client states' agreeing to refrain from building these facilities. A cautionary point is that many client states are concerned about relinquishing their asserted rights to all peaceful nuclear technologies, including enrichment and reprocessing. As discussed earlier, this "right" is contingent on a country maintaining adequate safeguards on its nuclear program and not seeking to acquire nuclear explosives. These states are thus most receptive to bilateral nuclear cooperation agreements that leave open the possibility of a state building enrichment or reprocessing facilities in the future. In this regard, the U.S. nuclear cooperation agreement with the United Arab Emirates is a useful precedent for future nuclear power development in the Middle East and other parts of the world; the emirates pledged to forgo developing national enrichment facilities as long as it is assured nuclear fuel from outside suppliers.

Another precedent for the future is Russia's insistence, before supplying fuel for the Bushehr reactor, on reaching an agreement with Iran to return the spent fuel to Russia, although the Iran-Russia agreement does not commit Iran to refrain from enriching its own uranium. Russia began offering such fuel-leasing services to client states during the Soviet era. Its fuel supply services and spent fuel take-back agreement with Iran supports the nonproliferation regime, and is a sound model for other states in a similar position. However, domestic political concerns have prevented the United States, France, and other fuel suppliers from making this offer. Their legislatures do not want to add to the volume of nuclear waste on their territories. No country has itself opened a permanent repository for high-level nuclear waste.

Another possible precedent involves programs, including the Global Threat Reduction Initiative, that facilitate the return of U.S.- and Russian-origin HEU spent fuel from research reactors. Although HEU spent fuel is small in weight, volume, and radioactivity content compared to commercial spent fuel, this program has illustrated the importance of removing materials that can pose a proliferation threat. In that respect, a fuel-leasing offer that includes spent fuel take-back has merit. However, any such offer would likely win support in Congress only if it were done for national security reasons. Similar to the structure of uranium enrichment assurances, spent fuel take-back offers will garner the support of both spent fuel recipients and spent fuel clients only if they are structured such that savings from not storing spent fuel in the client state pay for handling in the states storing it. A further incentive would be to include multiple partners that can safely and securely store spent fuel.

Security Practices and the Future of the U.S. Nuclear Weapons Complex

This chapter addresses two fundamental pillars of national and international systems to prevent the use of nuclear weapons: implementing best security practices and ensuring a safe, secure, and reliable U.S. nuclear arsenal. Any country with nuclear weapons and materials has the responsibility to maintain them with the highest security standards. But as this chapter makes clear, this security system needs to be strengthened further. The importance of implementing such a system cannot be overstated. Stronger security over nuclear weapons and materials is the most effective way to stop terrorists from gaining access to nuclear capabilities.

The second pillar provides the United States and its allies who depend on extended deterrence with high confidence in a credible nuclear deterrent. As discussed, credible extended deterrence helps reassure allies who may feel threatened by nuclear attacks that they do not need to acquire their own nuclear weapons. This pillar thus serves U.S. nonproliferation interests. However, a perception that the United States is seeking to add new nuclear missions, is lowering the nuclear threshold, or is maintaining a nuclear stockpile that is too large for U.S. and allied defense needs may erode support for the nonproliferation regime, especially among those allies and friends who believe strongly in working toward eventual nuclear disarmament. The Task Force underscores that transparency in intentions and actions and frequent consultations with allies about any proposed changes to the U.S. nuclear weapons complex serves U.S. interests.

NUCLEAR TERRORISM: WHY BETTER NUCLEAR SECURITY IS NEEDED

In the last three decades, mass casualty terrorism has grown. This tendency has been fueled by a number of factors, including the upsurge in religious extremism following the 1979 Islamic Revolution in Iran, state sponsorship of some mass casualty terrorism, and the increase in apocalyptic and millennial terrorist cults. To date, all acts of mass casualty terrorism have used conventional techniques, such as truck bombs, as well as airplane bombings and crashes to achieve high death tolls. Although most terrorist groups are not motivated to acquire or use weapons of mass destruction, some have used chemical and biological weapons. For example, Aum Shinrikyo, an apocalyptic cult headquartered in Japan, attacked the Tokyo subway system in 1995 with sarin gas, killing twelve and injuring more than a thousand people. In the 1990s, Aum Shinrikyo sought to acquire nuclear weapons. Similarly, al-Qaeda, which perpetrated the 9/11 attacks on New York and Washington, has been seeking to acquire nuclear and other weapons of mass destruction since the early 1990s. Without question, the United States faces the clear and present danger of terrorist enemies striving to obtain nuclear weapons.

Although terrorists face significant hurdles in trying to steal or buy either a nuclear bomb or the materials to construct an improvised nuclear device, this hugely consequential act cannot be ruled out.[68] If a reasonably technically skilled terrorist group acquired enough weapons-usable highly enriched uranium, it would likely be able to construct a gun-type nuclear bomb, which could compare to the destructive force of the Hiroshima bomb. Consequently, the Task Force underscores that blocking terrorist access to nuclear weapons and materials is an utmost priority.

A nuclear and radiation detection capability may complicate nuclear terrorist planning because it could force terrorists to use more radiation shielding to hide nuclear materials or convince them to employ alternate, and perhaps more complex, routes to deliver a nuclear explosive device to a target. The United States has been spending billions of dollars on nuclear and radiation detection equipment to try to interdict nuclear and radiological materials at borders and ports. It has also been working with other governments to increase intelligence sharing. Notably, along these lines, the George W. Bush administration launched the Proliferation Security Initiative and the Global Initiative to Combat Nuclear Terrorism, involving dozens of countries in such cooperative activities.

Traditional means of deterrence—in which an enemy's valued territory and assets are held at risk—are unlikely to work against stateless terrorist groups. Indirect deterrence, however, could help reduce the likelihood of nuclear weapons or weapons-usable materials falling into the hands of terrorists, especially by direct weapon or material transfers from states to terrorists. In particular, if the United States and its partners develop a stronger capability to attribute such weapons and materials to their countries of origin through nuclear forensics and other tools of attribution, those countries might be held accountable. But ensuring this accountability is challenging. Many experts agree, for instance, that greater focus on creating incentives for states to cooperate in sharing nuclear data with the United States is appropriate.[69] However, an overt or tacit threat of use of nuclear weapons against the countries of origin would decrease those countries' incentives to cooperate. Moreover, the U.S. ability to conduct attribution suffers from a lack of trained personnel and automated equipment.[70] U.S. leaders also need to better understand the scientific difficulties and inherent limitations in analyzing nuclear explosive debris and other forensic evidence to find the culprit of the attack and to recognize the relatively long time that nuclear forensics may require. Traditional law enforcement and intelligence assessments will also play a critical role in tracking down the perpetrators of a nuclear attack.

U.S. nuclear weapons have essentially no purpose in directly deterring stateless terrorist groups. To increase the likelihood of identifying the origin of fissile material that composes intercepted or detonated improvised nuclear devices, the United States should intensify international cooperative efforts to build a library of fissile material and increase domestic and international nuclear forensic capabilities, even though acting on nuclear forensic information entails significant political and technical uncertainties.

BEST SECURITY PRACTICES

With growing concerns about the transfer of nuclear materials to terrorists, the United States has increased its efforts domestically and internationally to improve the security of these materials. It has made major investments in improving the security of Russian nuclear weapons and nuclear materials and has led efforts through the IAEA to amend the Convention on Physical Protection of Nuclear Material (CPPNM) to strengthen its security requirements, to improve nuclear security in dozens of countries, and to support the work of the Nuclear Security Department of the International Atomic Energy Agency.

Nonetheless, much more work is needed. Despite trying to amend the CPPNM, governments have yet to agree on binding international security standards to boost security of weapons-usable nuclear material to the security of nuclear weapons themselves. The United States is one of the major donors to the IAEA's nuclear security fund, but this fund—at less than a few tens of millions of dollars annually—is starved for resources. It is important to recognize that the IAEA does not have a role to play in securing nuclear weapons or in developing best security practices for them. Primarily composed of nonnuclear weapon states, the IAEA is restricted in accessing design-related information on nuclear weapons. It does, however, have a significant role in assisting member states in developing best security practices on weapons-usable nuclear materials.

The Task Force urges the United States to redouble its and international efforts to achieve the entry into force of the amended CPPNM, to strengthen the IAEA's capabilities to work with member states to enhance nuclear security, and to establish and continue to improve global security standards for weapons-usable nuclear materials. Moreover, nonnuclear weapon states have a clear interest in implementing best security practices on their nuclear materials and making this issue a priority during the upcoming 2010 NPT Review Conference.

The Task Force welcomes the recent launch of the World Institute for Nuclear Security (WINS), which emerged from collaboration among the Nuclear Threat Initiative, the Institute for Nuclear Materials Management, and the U.S. Department of Energy's National Nuclear Security Administration, with the assistance of the IAEA. WINS "will bring together practitioners—the professionals responsible for on-the-ground security practices—to collect the world's best practices in nuclear materials security and to share that information with facilities that are responsible for protecting the world's most dangerous nuclear materials."[71] The strongest physical security of nuclear weapons-usable materials everywhere is in U.S. and global interests, and the Task Force urges the continued support of WINS by both government and private entities.

Concerning the security of nuclear weapons themselves, the United States has developed a number of methods to guard against both theft and unauthorized use. These include coded switches or permissive action links, unique signal generators that prevent stray electronic signals, noise, or interference from inadvertently arming the weapon, and environmental sensing devices that prevent detonation unless a specific sequence of external changes occurs (for example, particular accelerations during free fall of a gravity bomb). Reportedly, other countries have developed similar security methods, sometimes assisted by the United States.

Sharing the details of these methods raises security concerns (some such techniques are highly classified) and may pose legal problems under the NPT or U.S. nonproliferation law if shared with states other than nuclear weapons states under the NPT. Other areas of nuclear security cooperation are not nearly as sensitive. For instance, the United States has developed personnel reliability programs to monitor security guards and other people who have access to nuclear weapons to help ensure that they meet high standards of trustworthiness. The United States has also shared techniques of material protection, control, and accounting with Russia. Moreover, the United States can consider sharing its know-how on forming nuclear emergency search teams, which consist of specialists who can identify whether a terrorist threat to detonate a nuclear weapon is credible, and assess and defuse terrorists' improvised nuclear devices. The United States has a clear interest in sharing—to the extent possible—these nonsensitive security techniques.

In general, the United States and other nuclear-armed states can learn from each other in developing best security practices. Nonetheless, certain states are extremely reluctant to admit when they have had nuclear security lapses or breaches. Security discussions therefore need to be cautious about pointing to or even referring at all to specific incidents in the states in question. In many cases, it will be necessary to limit discussions to general principles and best practices (an approach the United States has taken with Russia). Where it appears desirable to be more explicit, nuclear-armed states could form a "buddy system" in which a state can work closely on security efforts with allied states. For example, China may feel most comfortable working with Pakistan, and the United States with the United Kingdom. Such a pairing of friends, however, does not remove the responsibility from the state itself in ensuring the physical security of its nuclear weapons and materials.

If the United States is to be effective in leading other states to improve nuclear security, its own practices must be—in fact and in perception—above reproach. The Bent Spear incident in August 2007, in which six U.S. nuclear-armed cruise missiles were flown across the United States without authorization, raised concerns about the effective administrative control of U.S. nuclear weapons. After investigating this incident, the Defense Science Board's permanent task force on nuclear weapons surety found that there was not "a clear understanding regarding who has explicit responsibility and accountability for any movement of special weapons outside the nuclear weapons storage area" and found "significant confusion about delegation of responsibility and authority for movement of nuclear weapons."[72] The bottom line, the investigation noted, was that "the decline in focus [of the nuclear enterprise] has been more pronounced than realized and too extreme to be acceptable."[73]

These concerns were confirmed by a Department of Defense task force on nuclear weapons management chaired by former secretary of defense James R. Schlesinger. The task force found that "there has been an unambiguous, dramatic, and unacceptable decline in the Air Force's commitment to perform the nuclear mission and, until very recently, little has been done to reverse it."[74] Both of these task forces made a number of specific recommendations for improvement, as did an internal Air Force investigation.[75] The Air Force subsequently adopted those recommendations.

Although there was no threat to the security of the nuclear weapons involved, this incident damaged the credibility of the United States and revealed significant procedural weaknesses. The seriousness with which it was taken, however, coupled with the openness of the investigations, can serve as an example to other states dealing with security problems. This is particularly true because the issues do not primarily result from the technical details of U.S. weapons, but rather from organizational and personnel failures that may have analogs in other countries. The government agencies involved in international nuclear security should use the lessons learned from the Bent Spear incident to improve global security practices.

In sum, the Task Force urges the United States to lead nuclear-armed states in establishing more effective security of nuclear weapons by discussing the evolving threat, evaluating the means to address the threat, and developing guidelines that all states with nuclear weapons would agree to implement.

CURRENT STATUS, RECENT REDUCTIONS, AND NEAR-FUTURE PROJECTIONS

Since the end of the Cold War, the United States has significantly reduced the number of land-, air-, and sea-based ballistic missile delivery systems. In particular, the United States has completely retired the MX/Peacekeeper ICBM system, which carried up to ten warheads per missile; retired the Minuteman II ICBM; reduced the number of Minuteman III ICBMs from five hundred to four hundred and fifty; and reduced the number of ballistic missile submarines (SSBNs) by converting four of the eighteen SSBNs existing at the end of the Cold War to nonnuclear weapons platforms. Reductions have been made in the number of warheads carried aboard those fourteen submarines and on the Minuteman III ICBMs. In addition, in October 1997, all B1-B bombers were relegated to conventional operations only and subsequently decertified for nuclear weapons. Moreover, shorter-range theater-based nuclear-capable systems have been reduced dramatically. As a direct result of President George H.W. Bush's initiatives in 1991 and 1992, the United States has eliminated most classes of these systems, with only an estimated several hundred remaining gravity bombs and nondeployed submarine-launched cruise missiles.

The United States has not built or deployed a new nuclear warhead since the end of the Cold War, when the W88 warhead entered service in 1990.[76] Although strategic delivery systems—Trident submarines, B-2 and B-52 bombers, and Minuteman III ICBMs—have not changed in outward appearance, the United States has continually modernized these platforms to make them more accurate and reliable and to extend their lifespan.

According to the Department of Defense and the Department of Energy, the United States is heading toward having the following strategic nuclear weapon delivery platforms in 2012: four hundred and fifty Minuteman III ICBMs, fourteen Ohio Class SSBNs (the majority of which are on active patrol at any given time), and twenty B-2 and fifty-six B-52 bombers. The November 2008 statement on this plan by the secretaries of these two departments noted that "this force structure allows the deployment of 1,700 to 2,200 warheads, provides flexibility to adjust the loading of warheads among the three legs of the triad in response to technical concerns or operational needs, and provides sufficient capacity to increase the number of deployed warheads in response to adverse geopolitical developments."[77]

In addition to deployed strategic warheads, the United States maintains a few thousand reserve, nondeployed warheads.[78] The November 2008 joint statement underscored that "because the United States does *not* have the ability to produce new warheads, a pool of non-deployed warheads is retained to be used in cases of reliability failures and as a hedge against adverse political developments."[79] Finally, the United States is estimated to have about five hundred warheads devoted to shorter-range weapon delivery systems, including Tomahawk submarine launched cruise missiles (none of which are deployed) and B61-3/4 tactical bombs.[80]

The Task Force strongly supports the substantial nuclear arms reductions that the United States has accomplished since the end of the Cold War and believes that the new administration, in the forthcoming nuclear posture review, has a strong interest in assessing what further reductions can be made by the United States alone and what reductions would need to occur in parallel with comparable Russian reductions.

DECOMMISSIONING AND DISMANTLING NUCLEAR WEAPONS

Reducing and eliminating nuclear weapons means considerably more than transferring deployed nuclear warheads from military units to a secure storage facility. Eliminating the destructive potential of the weapon requires a systematic process to decommission and dismantle retired devices. This process proceeds through several stages: decommissioning the weapon and transferring it to storage or reserve status; dismantling the weapon, including separating high explosives from the nuclear material and destroying the fusing and weapon housing; storing and breaking up the plutonium pit and other nuclear material components, such as highly enriched uranium in the secondary thermonuclear part of the weapon; and ultimately transforming the plutonium and other weapons-usable fissile material in reactors or other devices to make them unusable in nuclear weapons.

At each stage of the process, it is progressively more difficult to reconstitute a nuclear weapon. The spectrum of potential weaponization is completely avoided only after the strategic nuclear material is destroyed.

Current U.S. efforts focus on increasing the pace of dismantlement. This is complicated by the fact, as mentioned early in this report, that the same facility—the Pantex plant in Texas—that dismantles warheads for elimination also disassembles and reassembles warheads for routine surveillance or life extensions. Thus, there is an inherent tension between dismantling the large number of weapons authorized for retirement and maintaining the current stockpile. In recent years, the National Nuclear Security Administration (NNSA), a semiautonomous agency within the Department of Energy, has significantly increased the rate of processing warheads at the Pantex plant, which is now essentially operating at maximum capacity.[81]

At present, the United States must retain the plutonium pits from retired weapons, pending the construction of facilities to eliminate excess plutonium. Although some excess HEU will be blended down for use in commercial reactors, most will be retained to meet future demands for fuel for the Navy's nuclear-powered submarines and aircraft carriers. This plan will preclude for more than half a century any need to produce HEU for propelling military ships.

A proper assessment of progress on reducing or eliminating nuclear weapons requires consideration of each stage of the process. Relatively little information is available about the status or cost of decommissioning the retired nuclear weapons inventory of the United States or of other countries. Secrecy about the size and character of a nuclear weapons inventory gives rise to suspicion about the reality of weapons reductions—that is, how easily retired weapons could be returned to operational status. Transparency is therefore needed to establish confidence about the character of nuclear weapons stockpiles and the progress toward effective reductions.

The Task Force believes that increased transparency about its nuclear weapons inventory advances U.S. nonproliferation objectives by setting an international standard. In particular, the United States should reveal in a public statement the numbers and type of weapons awaiting dismantlement.

The United States has a strong interest in accelerating the pace of dismantlement of its several thousand retired warheads to demonstrate leadership in reducing possible security risks of excess warheads. However, because of the dual nature of the Pantex warhead processing facility, the United States faces a dilemma: slow down life extensions on the remaining warheads or speed up dismantlement of the retired warheads. The Task Force urges that any warheads scheduled for dismantlement should irreversibly remain in that status and that the United States should study, as part of the 2009 nuclear posture review, whether and how to accelerate the process of dismantling retired warheads.

ENSURING SAFE, SECURE, AND RELIABLE U.S. NUCLEAR WEAPONS

As long as the United States has nuclear weapons, it must maintain confidence in their safety, security, and reliability. The nuclear weapons complex helps provide that confidence. It consists of three nuclear weapons laboratories, four production facilities, and the Nevada Test Site (all operated by the NNSA); nuclear weapons launching systems, including submarines, land-based ballistic missiles, long-range bombers, and aircraft for short-range nuclear weapons; and the command and control systems that link these platforms with higher authorities (all operated by the Department of Defense, and several other supporting Department of Energy and Department of Defense facilities).

During the Cold War, the nuclear weapons complex was continuously developing and producing new weapons, with underground nuclear testing providing a major tool for understanding weapons performance. This system ensured a continuous supply of weapons designers, who learned their craft through an apprenticeship system, and passed along much of its knowledge through tacit learning between senior weapon scientists and their junior colleagues.[82] Because many of these senior scientists have retired in recent years, and because their younger colleagues do not have experience with the development cycle for a new weapon or with nuclear testing, there are concerns about ensuring the highest caliber workforce at the weapons laboratories.

The Cold War nuclear arms race featured the frequent replacement of weapons with newer designs. As a result, concern about component aging and its long-term effect on the reliability of particular designs was minimal. With the end of the Cold War, however, the continuous design and deployment cycle that had organized the weapons program ceased abruptly. Further, in 1992, the United States imposed an indefinite moratorium on underground nuclear testing. The weapons community was faced with a need to maintain and certify the long-term reliability of the stockpile without testing or replacements planned for any existing weapons.

The weapons labs responded to this challenge by creating the Stockpile Stewardship Program and the warhead Life Extension Program. Stockpile Stewardship (initially called Science-Based Stockpile Stewardship) used a combination of nonnuclear experiments (many involving new scientific tools, such as advanced radiography), subcritical experiments (involving nuclear materials but not producing nuclear yield), careful reassessment of previous nuclear tests, and increases in computing power of over a millionfold to provide assessments of the nuclear performance of existing weapons in the absence of nuclear testing. The Life Extension Program involved the major refurbishment of various warhead types with the aim of restoring them to an as-built condition. One of the goals of Stockpile Stewardship was to ensure that the inevitable small changes that accumulate from warhead refurbishment did not affect nuclear performance.

To date, the Stockpile Stewardship Program and the warhead Life Extension Program have had remarkable success and, in turn, have provided confidence in the safety and reliability of the arsenal since the U.S. nuclear testing moratorium began in 1992. Each subsequent year, the secretaries of defense and energy, based on input from the three weapons laboratory directors and the commander of U.S. Strategic Command (STRATCOM), have formally certified that the stockpile remains safe, secure, and reliable, and that a resumption of nuclear testing is not required. Based on these certifications, the George W. Bush administration continued the moratorium even as it opposed ratification of the Comprehensive Test Ban Treaty.

During the first term of the Bush administration, the directors of the three weapons laboratories expressed growing concern over the long-term ability of Stockpile Stewardship to allow the continued certification of the stockpile. They cautioned that uncertainties in performance due to component aging and the small changes introduced during refurbishment of aging components could grow faster than the ability of the Stockpile Stewardship Program to understand those uncertainties.[83] In 2005, following informal briefings on this concept, Representative David Hobson (R-OH) and Senator Pete Domenici (R-NM) introduced legislation to have the weapons labs research a new warhead, called the reliable replacement warhead (RRW).[84] Their intention, like that of the

Bush administration, was not to have the RRW take on new military missions but instead to hedge against the failure of Cold War legacy warheads. In addition, because the United States has not built a new warhead since the late 1980s, research on RRW would help maintain essential warhead design and engineering capabilities at the national laboratories. Both Congress and the Bush administration made it clear that RRW would be developed and fielded only if it could be done without resorting to underground nuclear testing. Despite this, some critics are concerned that the Department of Defense would require the RRW to be tested to induct this weapon system into the military, thereby opening the door for other countries to test and thus improve their own nuclear capabilities.

The RRW is related to a larger proposed mission to transform the nuclear weapons complex. On December 16, 2008, NNSA issued two records of decision for this transformation.[85] Proponents claim that the ultimate transformation will save the United States billions of dollars and significantly reduce the footprint of the entire complex. However, critics are concerned that the parallel implementation of stockpile stewardship and complex transformation will be unaffordable, given likely budget constraints, and will result in unacceptable cuts to the science programs at the weapons laboratories. Some critics also believe that decisions on complex transformation are premature until more fundamental issues of nuclear policy are resolved.

The Task Force believes the following principles should guide the Obama administration in its decision making on complex transformation and proposals on replacement warheads:

- The United States needs to have continued high confidence that its warheads are safe, secure, and reliable, and that the nuclear weapons complex is optimizing cost savings while meeting its mission.

- Although the Stockpile Stewardship Program and the Life Extension Program have maintained the U.S. government's confidence for two decades that U.S. warheads are safe, secure, and reliable, a detailed cost-benefit analysis on the aging of all legacy warhead components, both their nuclear and nonnuclear parts, and on any proposals for developing and building replacement warheads, would provide a basis for making a sound decision. This examination is critical in an era of economic crisis.

– The weapons labs need to exercise the talents of scientific, engineering, and managerial staff. Although design work has already begun on replacement warheads, the involved personnel need to be challenged to continue investigations on other potential warhead designs, ways to counter nuclear and nonnuclear weapons that can be used by terrorists, and the verification issues surrounding warhead dismantlement.

– Any new warhead designs should meet four criteria: no required new nuclear testing, no additional military capabilities, enhanced safety and security features, and enough confidence in the designs and manufacturing processes to allow for deep reductions in reserve warheads.

MANAGING THE NUCLEAR WEAPONS COMPLEX

Effective management of the nuclear weapons enterprise is a prerequisite for effective nuclear policy. In 2000, Congress created the National Nuclear Security Administration within the Department of Energy. Some believe that NNSA does not have enough autonomy and has not been as effective as necessary. The resulting proposed remedy is that NNSA and its stockpile management responsibility should be taken out of the Department of Energy and either transferred to the Department of Defense or established as an independent agency.

The Task Force notes that the organizational location of the agency responsible for managing the weapons complex is not critical to U.S. nuclear policy or to the size and composition of the nuclear forces necessary to support that policy. The Task Force has therefore not considered possible modifications to the NNSA authorizing legislation, but is extremely skeptical of any proposal to transfer the weapons program to the Department of Defense for the following reasons.

First, the current arrangements provide for effective input from the Department of Defense. The Department of Defense Strategic Command and Nuclear Weapons Council are the decisive voices in setting requirements for the Department of Energy's nuclear weapons program. These mechanisms are intended to ensure that the Department of Energy weapons complex is responsive to defense needs, and that budget trade-offs are considered.

Second, the secretary of defense already has extraordinarily broad managerial responsibilities. Transferring the weapons complex to the Department of Defense would not necessarily result in better senior civilian management oversight or in great efficiency of operation. Indeed, such a transfer could make it easier to slight long-term needs in favor of short-term priorities. Further, some believe that the Department of Defense is not as well suited as the Department of Energy to manage science laboratories.

Third, such a transfer would eliminate the independent voices in the process of annual stockpile certification that come from involving two separate agencies.

Fourth, the transfer would further separate nuclear weapons activities from the management of defense-related nuclear waste.

Finally, the three major weapons laboratories, Los Alamos, Livermore, and Sandia, are called national laboratories because their significant technology base has contributed and should be expected to contribute to many missions, including nonnuclear defense needs, nonproliferation, homeland security, intelligence support, energy research and development, and basic science. Integrating these laboratories into the Department of Defense would make these missions more difficult to support.

Thus, the Task Force would oppose any transfer of the stockpile management program or the National Nuclear Security Administration to the Department of Defense.

Recommendations

The Task Force believes strongly in a nuclear security system in which rights come with responsibilities. All states have the responsibility to ensure that nuclear weapons are never used again, to prevent the further spread of nuclear weapons and nuclear weapons capabilities to more states, and to block terrorist access to nuclear weapons and weapons-usable materials. Under the theme of responsible nuclear security, the recommendations are framed in terms of the following principles and objectives:

– reenergizing functioning and communicative political relationships with major nuclear-armed powers, with emphasis on strategic dialogue with Russia and China as well as the objective of a new legally binding and verifiable arms control agreement between the United States and Russia;

– preventing the proliferation of nuclear weapons and know-how to additional states and nonstate actors by boosting the health of the international nuclear nonproliferation regime;

– reaffirming and maintaining U.S. extended deterrence commitments to allies;

– ensuring that the U.S. nuclear stockpile is safe, secure, and reliable to maintain the credibility of the U.S. nuclear deterrent; and

– implementing best security practices for nuclear weapons and weapons-usable materials worldwide to prevent unauthorized access and loss of control to nonstate actors such as terrorist groups.

STRATEGIC DIALOGUE AND ARMS CONTROL

Political relationships fundamentally matter in reducing the likelihood of nuclear weapons use. Obviously, an intentional nuclear war is far more likely to occur with an ideological foe than with a nuclear-armed friend. Specifically, the demise of the Soviet Union in 1991 most certainly lowered the prospects of nuclear war between the United States and Russia, the main Soviet successor state. A major strategic miscalculation, however, could conceivably lead to the use of nuclear weapons. Almost twenty years after the end of the Cold War, Russia remains a state in transition and continues to exert power over its traditional sphere of influence. In particular, the war between Georgia and Russia in 2008 has worried some American politicians and analysts that Russia may revert to Cold War practices. Russia perceives itself in a position of conventional inferiority and military encirclement in respect to the United States and NATO. Consequently, Moscow has maintained tactical nuclear weapon systems for possible war fighting roles, expressed opposition to NATO enlargement to include Georgia and Ukraine, opposed deployment of a U.S. missile defense system in the Czech Republic and Poland, announced plans to begin large-scale military modernization by 2011, and expressed concern about prompt global strike conventional arms, such as the potential arming of the U.S. Trident submarine missile with conventional munitions, citing perceived threats to Russia's nuclear deterrent and the potential for strategic miscalculation.

Despite these apparent impediments, Moscow has usually shown strong interest in nuclear arms control. Russia and the United States have a special responsibility in the nuclear arena. They were the first two nuclear-armed states and the first two countries to commercialize nuclear energy. They both have an additional vested interest in nonproliferation, having joined political forces in the 1960s to push for the enactment of the NPT in 1970.

Although the Bush administration discussed these impediments and areas of common interest with the Putin and Medvedev administrations, the two sides did not resolve the impasse over next steps. The Obama administration has an opportunity for a fresh start with Russia. The Task Force offers the following advice:

- Premise renewed strategic dialogue between the United States and Russia on the common interests of preventing the use of nuclear weapons, strengthening the nonproliferation regime, securing nuclear material worldwide, and increasing the prospects of safe and secure use of peaceful nuclear energy.

– Provide for a START-type legal and verification foundation for uninterrupted regulation, transparency, and predictability for U.S. and Russian nuclear forces while negotiating a follow-on treaty to START and SORT.

– Negotiate a legally binding follow-on treaty on strategic weapons that would reflect current defense needs and realities and would result in deeper arms reductions. The Task Force does not want to prejudge the actual magnitude of reductions or other changes in nuclear posture. Instead, the Task Force underscores the value of first having meaningful strategic dialogue between the United States and Russia about threat assessments and perceived defense needs.

– Include, as an important part of strategic dialogue, discussions on missile defense, nondeployed warheads, nonstrategic nuclear forces, and prompt conventional strike weapons. (Deeper reductions beyond what will likely be agreed on for the immediate post-SORT agreement will hinge on the understanding developed through these discussions.)

– Be transparent about U.S. intentions and capabilities. Work cooperatively to ensure unimpeded situational awareness, given the fundamental link between transparency and crisis stability. Implement the Joint Data Exchange Center promptly.

– Delay ballistic missile defense deployments in Europe until this defense system is technically viable and shown to be needed. Equally important, perform a joint missile threat assessment. (The proposed missile defense system is being designed to counter an emerging Iranian ballistic missile threat. More effective coordinated efforts between the United States and Russia, in cooperation with European allies and China, to resolve the Iranian nuclear threat could preclude deployment of a missile defense system in Europe.)

– Build on the success of the Cooperative Threat Reduction Program, other cooperative threat reduction programs such as the Warhead Safety and Security Exchange agreement, the Global Threat Reduction Initiative, and the Megatons-to-Megawatts agreement to achieve better security of and much larger reductions in weapons-usable nuclear materials. (CTR began in 1992 and has provided substantial assistance to Russia and former Soviet successor states, and was recently extended to other states, to secure weapons of mass destruction and the materials to make those weapons. The challenge and opportunity now is to transform the various cooperative threat reduction programs into a true partnership between the United States and Russia.)

– Revitalize nuclear warhead safety and security programs through an umbrella agreement that would allow U.S. and Russian experts to work jointly to develop new technical approaches to arms control verification, nonproliferation, and counterterrorism.

– Develop a new approach or agreement with Russia to convert hundreds of additional tons of weapons-grade Russian uranium into nonweapons-usable nuclear fuel. (The Megatons-to-Megawatts agreement started in 1995 to convert five hundred metric tons of weapons-grade Russian uranium—enough material to make twenty thousand nuclear warheads—into nonweapons-usable nuclear reactor fuel. This material has been fueling half of all U.S. nuclear power plants, providing approximately 10 percent of the electricity generated in the United States. The conversion of this weapons-origin uranium is set to be completed by the end of 2013. It is estimated that Russia has hundreds of more tons of weapons-grade uranium. Russia would likely object to continuing the terms of this agreement, however. Thus, when negotiating a new agreement, the United States should listen anew to Russian concerns and integrate the interests of the commercial nuclear industry.)

Although the U.S.-Russia relationship is ripe for a new formal arms control agreement, the U.S.-China relationship is not, given the current large asymmetry between U.S. and Chinese nuclear forces. The rise of China as a global economic power, however, the modernization of China's nuclear forces, the imperative to cooperate on a new security architecture for East Asia in anticipation of eventual Korean reunification, mutual interests with respect to nonproliferation, and the 2007 test of a Chinese antisatellite weapon are all ample reasons why the United States and China should develop a much better strategic understanding. In particular, Chinese nuclear force modernization is likely driven in part by its concerns about the current and future capabilities and intentions of the United States, including missile defense. China has also resisted announcing a formal halt to the production of fissile material for nuclear weapons. As with the U.S.-Russia strategic dialogue, a U.S.-China nuclear and strategic dialogue must begin with a clear explanation of each side's interests and concerns. The Task Force further recommends the following steps for the United States:

- Conduct frequent military-to-military discussions with China on nuclear security issues.

- Be transparent with China about U.S. intentions and capabilities with missile defense. Offer an agreement for formal transparency and confidence-building measures on this issue.

- Propose a trilateral ban with China and Russia on tests of kinetic antisatellite weapons that can destroy both civilian and military satellites with projectiles fired from land-, air-, or space-based launching systems. Discuss with China and Russia how to expand such a ban to the global level and the broader issue of space weapons.

NONPROLIFERATION

Failure to resolve the Iranian and North Korean proliferation challenges could lead to more states acquiring nuclear weapons or the capabilities to make those weapons. The more states there are with nuclear weapons, the more likely it is that these weapons will be used either intentionally or through strategic miscalculation, or suffer loss of control. An increase in the number of states with nuclear weapons or weapons-usable materials also heightens the risk of terrorist access to these stockpiles.

The Task Force emphasizes that the most effective way to prevent nuclear terrorism is to reduce the amounts and availability of weapons-usable nuclear material—whether in weapons programs or civilian applications—and to provide the highest standards of security for what remains. In particular, as the United States and Russia take further steps to dismantle their nuclear weapons, they should ensure that the fissile material removed from these weapons is either processed as quickly as possible into nonweapons-usable form or is subject to the strongest security measures while in weapons-usable form.

Iran poses the toughest proliferation challenge. Under the guise of a peaceful nuclear program, the Iranian authorities have been obtaining the latent ability to make nuclear weapons. At present (early 2009), the Iranian uranium enrichment program is capable of producing at least one weapon's worth of highly enriched uranium within a few months, if Tehran were to decide to leave the NPT or operate a clandestine nuclear weapons program in further violation of its safeguards agreement with the IAEA. Iran has defied UN Security Council resolutions to suspend its uranium enrichment program. The Obama administration hopes to address these challenges by opening a dialogue with Iran based on mutual interests and respect, and employing all available tools to resolve the impasse.

Given the scope of this report, the Task Force has focused on strengthening the nonproliferation regime as a way to contain the Iranian proliferation threat, rather than deliberate the possible political and military solutions to this problem. A nuclear-armed or even a nuclear-weapons-capable Iran might lead other nations in the Middle East and surrounding regions to acquire their own nuclear weapons or the capabilities to readily make them. In recent years, about a dozen countries in these regions have expressed interest in nuclear power programs. Although the acquisition of nuclear power plants alone would not present a serious danger of proliferation, it could eventually lead these countries toward uranium enrichment and reprocessing of spent nuclear fuel to separate plutonium—both weapons-usable technologies—unless these countries have incentives not to pursue these technologies.

The administration will have to act quickly to prepare for the May 2010 NPT Review Conference, a major opportunity to lead international efforts in strengthening the nuclear security system. In this area, the Task Force urges the Obama administration to lead and work cooperatively with others by undertaking the following steps:

– Prepare a high-level diplomatic team, as soon as possible, for the lead-up to the conference. The administration has already formally announced the nomination of a U.S. special representative of the president to the conference and designated this post as ambassadorial in rank, both promising signs. Before the conference, this team should meet with high-level foreign government officials to elevate the level of focus on the NPT in foreign capitals away from "nonproliferation diplomats" to senior officials who can best appreciate how the NPT increases their overall national security. The United States should generally emphasize the theme that the rights given to any NPT member are contingent on the member honoring its commitments and responsibilities under the treaty.

- Ensure that countries with nuclear power plants are provided with multiple assurances of nuclear fuel supplies, through the existing market, political commitments, insurance coverage, and fuel banks, to demonstrate a reduced incentive to build national uranium enrichment facilities. The United States should work with existing uranium enrichment suppliers to determine whether and how to supply nuclear fuel in a cost-neutral way such that the cost of production equals the price paid by clients, so as to remove the perceived economic benefit of becoming a fuel supplier and thus to further decrease the incentive for additional states to build their own enrichment plants.

- Freeze the construction of new nationally owned and operated uranium enrichment plants. Any new plants should require international ownership, with personnel and physical security measures implemented at the plants to prevent unauthorized access or transfer of enrichment technologies.

- Set up a fuel-leasing program that would allow the United States to reduce the risk of a state reprocessing spent fuel to separate plutonium by accepting spent nuclear fuel from states that have newly acquired nuclear power plants. Although Congress may at first balk at such a proposal because of constituents' concerns about accepting foreign nuclear waste, the Task Force notes that the George W. Bush administration's Global Threat Reduction Initiative accepted U.S.-origin research reactor spent fuel containing highly enriched uranium to preclude its theft. The new administration has expressed interest in continuing the GTRI. The Task Force also recommends that the Obama administration encourage Russia to continue its policy of requiring the repatriation of spent fuel, as it did Iran regarding spent fuel from the Bushehr nuclear power plant.

- Make the Additional Protocol, a more rigorous application of IAEA safeguards, a prerequisite for states to obtain commercial nuclear power technologies. These states must also demonstrate that they are fully compliant with their existing safeguards agreements. The Additional Protocol, however, has some gaps. It does not prevent states from building clandestine nuclear facilities. Also, in states with a good track record with the nonproliferation regime, the number of inspections is reduced as a cost-cutting measure for the IAEA. The IAEA needs adequate analytic and inspection resources to periodically monitor all states with significant nuclear power programs regardless of compliance record.

– Develop and implement more effective safeguards techniques, including wide-area environmental sampling and near-real-time monitoring of nuclear facilities, including by U.S. intelligence agencies. Work with and encourage the IAEA's board of governors to have advanced safeguards techniques adopted as universal standards.

– Provide increased and sustainable funding to the IAEA's safeguards and nuclear security departments to match the increased use of nuclear power and increased amount of nuclear material. Because safeguards and nuclear security activities are often looked on as a burden by developing states, there is a corresponding need to ensure that the IAEA's technical cooperation budget is commensurately increased. A state's assessed contribution to these budgets should be proportionate to their use of peaceful nuclear power.

– Correct weaknesses in the NPT that permit a state to leave the treaty while under violation of its safeguards agreement. The Task Force recognizes and supports the supreme national interest clause allowing a state to exit the NPT or other arms control treaties, but it cautions that a state could use this clause as a loophole to exit the treaty while under strong suspicion of developing a nuclear weapons program. Having enjoyed the benefits of the NPT, a withdrawing state found in violation of its safeguards agreement should be required to return to the countries of origin the nuclear materials and technologies it obtained while a member of the treaty. In addition, the UN Security Council should seek to conduct a special inspection of that state to determine whether any safeguarded materials or technologies have been used in weapons programs. The Task Force acknowledges that the United States or the UN Security Council cannot coerce or otherwise force a state to remain inside the NPT and that it would be difficult to enforce these proposed measures.

– Increase national and international efforts toward entry into force of the Comprehensive Test Ban Treaty, which would ban nuclear testing worldwide. While a state could develop a first-generation Hiroshima-type nuclear bomb without nuclear testing, the CTBT would prevent a state from gaining guaranteed technical assurance through nuclear testing that advanced nuclear weapons would work reliably. The political benefit of the CTBT is that it has been strongly linked to the vitality of the nonproliferation regime. The Task Force believes that the benefits outweigh the costs and that the CTBT is in U.S. national security interests. The Senate should consider additional safeguards, including a more effective nuclear stockpile refurbishment program. The Senate should also consider requiring the executive branch to provide a detailed report at least every four years on whether the CTBT continues to serve U.S. interests. If and when the Senate ratifies the CTBT, the United States should redouble efforts to work with allies to urge remaining holdout states of China, Egypt, India, Indonesia, Iran, Israel, North Korea, and Pakistan to ratify this treaty and help secure its entry into force.

– Redouble international efforts to phase out highly enriched uranium in civilian applications, such as in research reactors, isotope production reactors, and icebreakers. HEU is the nuclear material that is the easiest to use to make an improvised nuclear device, the type of nuclear explosive that terrorists would most likely try to build. The Global Threat Reduction Initiative has reduced the use of HEU in research and isotope production reactors. As part of this initiative, the United States worked cooperatively with Russia and dozens of other countries to repatriate Soviet-origin HEU to Russia and U.S.-origin HEU to the United States. The program has also led to the conversion of many reactors from HEU to nonweapons-usable low-enriched uranium. However, although the United States has converted most of its HEU-fueled reactors to LEU, Russia has yet to convert any of its dozens of HEU-fueled isotope-production, research, and test reactors. Overcoming Russian resistance to converting its reactors is a challenge for the Obama administration. Incentives to reduce Russia's use of civilian HEU should include financial assistance to decommission older HEU-using facilities, the involvement of Russian nuclear scientists in research activities that do not involve use of HEU, and, as a transitional objective, the consolidation of dozens of such reactors and critical assemblies into a handful with enhanced security features.

– Demonstrate through transparency of intentions and actions that the United States has taken significant steps toward reducing its nuclear stockpile, and affirm during the conference that it will continue to make a good-faith effort—called for by Article VI of the NPT—to pursue nuclear disarmament. President Obama has said that "as long as nuclear weapons exist, we'll retain a strong deterrent. But we'll make the goal of eliminating all nuclear weapons a central element in our nuclear policy." Concerns remain, however, that complete nuclear disarmament is neither feasible nor desirable. To this end, the United States should ask for and determine the views of other states as to what political and security conditions as well as verification procedures would be necessary to abolish nuclear weapons.

– Call for a global moratorium on the production of fissile material for weapons purposes before the conference. The Obama administration offering this proposal would not by itself convince China, India, Israel, and Pakistan—the major holdout states—to support a fissile material cutoff. Nonetheless, the administration should leverage this call for action to rally many allies to support the strengthening of the nonproliferation regime. Also, the Task Force recognizes that the mechanism of the Conference on Disarmament has led to a stalemated discussion on the proposed Fissile Material Cutoff Treaty. The Task Force therefore urges the administration to try to gain better traction by initiating parallel discussions with the aforementioned states. Moreover, the Obama administration should reexamine the previous administration's conclusion that there are no appropriate verification provisions for the FMCT. The Task Force believes that the United States should treat the FMCT, though it is an important initiative, as a lower priority than the CTBT at the conference.

EXTENDED DETERRENCE

The United States does not need nuclear weapons to compensate for conventional military inferiority and has no reason to fear a conventionally armed foe. But U.S. allies, including members of the NATO alliance, Australia, Japan, and South Korea, depend on security assurances from the United States. A component of these assurances is protection against nuclear attack. U.S. nuclear weapons represent one facet of multilayered defenses—including diplomacy, economic support, and conventional military forces—that deter attacks and defend allies in the event of an attack. Without the nuclear aspect of these assurances, some U.S. allies may decide in the future to acquire nuclear weapons. The Task Force strongly supports maintaining and enhancing, where necessary, U.S. security assurances to allies. With respect to the nuclear aspect of these assurances, the Task Force advises the Obama administration to undertake the following steps:

–   Reaffirm U.S. commitment to security assurances, including extended nuclear deterrence, to allies.

–   Consult with allies to determine their views about the credibility of the nuclear role in security assurances to assess whether any adjustments in nuclear and conventional capabilities are necessary.

–   Keep the relatively small U.S. nuclear stockpile in Europe as long as this force supports NATO political objectives in reassuring allies and acts as a disincentive for NATO allies to build their own nuclear forces.

CREDIBLE NUCLEAR DETERRENT

A credible U.S. nuclear deterrent depends on maintaining a safe, secure, and reliable nuclear arsenal, including warheads and weapon delivery systems. As long as the United States maintains nuclear weapons, it must ensure that the weapons complex has enough human and technical resources. In recent years, however, concerns have been raised about the long-term viability of the nuclear weapons complex. Since 1992, when the United States last conducted a nuclear test, the weapons labs and the associated material and manufacturing facilities have applied the Stockpile Stewardship Program and the Life Extension Program to maintain legacy nuclear warheads from the Cold War. The United States has not designed or built a new warhead since the Cold War. Each strategic weapon delivery system has two types of warheads it can use, and the United States has been maintaining several thousand reserve warheads. The United States spends several billion dollars annually on stockpile stewardship. These conditions have led to three major concerns: how to attract top scientific talent to the weapons labs in an era of no nuclear testing and no development of new warheads, how to transform the weapons complex to save substantial costs in the long term and to create the conditions for substantial reductions in reserve warheads, and how to ensure the safety, security, and reliability of the remaining warheads and delivery systems.

In recent years, one of the most controversial proposals has been to build the reliable replacement warhead. Proponents claim that the RRW would include advanced safety and security features and other measures to ensure reliability without creating additional military capabilities or requiring nuclear testing. To improve workers' safety, it would also reduce the amount of toxic materials as compared to the components in legacy warheads. The Los Alamos and Lawrence Livermore labs have undergone a design competition for a proposed replacement warhead. However, the RRW has not been authorized for development or even for a cost-and-feasibility study. Congress stated that such action was premature until more fundamental policy questions were addressed. Some critics are concerned that the military will not have confidence in these warheads absent testing and, in turn, that U.S. testing would open the door for other nuclear-armed states to test. They also worry that the development of the RRW may be perceived by other states as a new weapons system and thus undermine U.S. efforts to rally support among many allies for strengthening the nonproliferation regime. President Obama has stated that his administration will not develop new nuclear weapons, and Secretary Gates has been on the record as supporting the RRW.[86] The Task Force offers the following guidance on the nuclear weapons complex:

- Ensure that the stockpile stewardship program has the resources and talent it needs to maintain the safety, security, and reliability of the remaining warheads in the arsenal.

- Maintain a readiness to modernize or replace the U.S. arsenal, including weapon delivery systems, dating from the Cold War, as necessary.

- Be transparent about any proposed changes to the nuclear weapons complex. This means that any decision for or against a particular program, such as the reliable replacement warhead, should be coupled with vigorous diplomatic outreach to allies to explain clearly why these decisions were made.

- Couple decisions about proposed weapons complex changes to a rigorous assessment of the future roles of U.S. nuclear weapons and strategic dialogue with Russia and China.

- Conduct a comprehensive cost-benefit assessment of proposals to transform the weapons complex. This assessment is vital in an era of economic crisis.

– Implement an integrated approach to weapons complex transformation that assesses the full range of nuclear security activities. That is, the Task Force supports a nuclear weapons security enterprise that stresses the equal importance of nonproliferation, prevention of nuclear terrorism, maintenance of a credible nuclear arsenal, and steps toward nuclear disarmament.

– Do not move nuclear warhead maintenance responsibilities or the management of the Department of Energy's National Nuclear Security Administration to the Department of Defense.

– Exercise the intellectual capacity of the technically talented people at the weapons labs, including rigorous investigations into countering terrorists' weapons, both nuclear and nonnuclear. Renew lab research on the verification challenges of ensuring dismantlement of other countries' nuclear warheads.

BEST SECURITY PRACTICES

A country with nuclear weapons or weapons-usable nuclear materials has a special responsibility to protect them against unauthorized access or other loss of control. Because terrorist groups without state assistance are unlikely to have the means to produce fissile material for nuclear weapons, they would have to target state-produced stockpiles, whether in the military or civilian sectors, to make a nuclear device. Terrorists could also try to steal intact nuclear weapons. It is essential, therefore, to implement best security practices. The Task Force supports the pledge made during the presidential campaign by then presidential candidate Obama to "secure all loose nuclear materials in the world within four years."

The Task Force finds that though many places worldwide require additional nuclear security, the situation in Pakistan is in need of particular attention. Many of the terrorists who seek nuclear weapons or fissile material are especially active in Pakistan and the surrounding region. In addition, because Pakistan has a history of political instability and has based its weapons program mainly on highly enriched uranium, which can be used most easily to make nuclear devices, the Task Force urges the Obama administration to redouble efforts to work with Pakistan to improve nuclear security. Islamabad, meanwhile, has been wary of assistance that might reveal sensitive information about the designs and locations of its nuclear weapons or that might publicly suggest that it is beholden to Washington for nuclear security. With respect to these concerns, the Task Force recommends that the United States offer, if it has not already done so, security cooperation that includes generic physical security procedures, unclassified military handbooks, portal control equipment, sophisticated vaults and access doors, and personnel reliability programs, while striving to not increase the likelihood of nuclear war in South Asia, harm relations with India, or undermine the Pakistani government. Similarly, because of terrorist activities in India, the United States should work with New Delhi in a cooperative manner to share lessons learned about developing best security practices.

The United States itself has recently taken action to ensure authorized control of its nuclear weapons. In August 2007, the U.S. Air Force did not exercise adequate control over six nuclear-armed cruise missiles that were flown across the United States without proper authorization. Secretary Gates acted quickly and appropriately to instill better discipline and professionalism in the Air Force's nuclear command. The Task Force recommends that the United States applies the lessons learned from this incident to its cooperative global work in improving accountability over nuclear weapons and weapons-usable materials.

In the issue area of implementing best security practices, the Task Force calls on the Obama administration to undertake the following steps:

- Hold a presidential summit with Russian president Medvedev to secure a joint U.S.-Russia commitment to lead global efforts to implement best nuclear security practices. This summit will build and expand on the Bush-Putin summit held in Bratislava in February 2005, in which both Russia and the United States committed to strengthen cooperative efforts to counter nuclear terrorism.
- Follow through on President Obama's pledge to convene a global conference within the first year of the administration on nuclear terrorism prevention. This conference will provide an opportunity to convince all states with nuclear weapons-usable materials to implement best security practices within the president's goal date of 2012.

- Implement expeditiously the National Nuclear Security Administration's action plan to secure and remove, where feasible, weapons-usable nuclear materials, especially highly enriched uranium at dozens of sites worldwide.

- Increase transparency about the status of the U.S. nuclear weapons inventory. The purpose of this policy is to set an international standard for reporting on nuclear weapons status—thereby encouraging other nations to do the same. This would reinforce the importance of accountability and stewardship of all weapons in a nation's possession.

- Commit the United States to publishing an annual report detailing its nuclear dismantlement activities, including the number and type of warheads formally retired and awaiting dismantlement. The United States should encourage other nuclear-armed nations to report on their progress in these efforts.

- Increase, as much as possible, the rate at which U.S. nuclear warheads slated for dismantlement are disassembled.

- Dispose of fissile material, including highly enriched uranium and plutonium, in excess of U.S. defense needs into nonweapons-usable forms and provide high security for the retained material.

- Share as much information as possible, consistent with legal and classification requirements, with other nuclear-armed states, to encourage equipping all nuclear weapons with mechanisms and procedures to prevent unauthorized use.

- Share lessons learned from the United States' own security lapses—in confidential discussions—as an important step in encouraging the highest standards of nuclear custodianship.

- Work with member states of the IAEA to move the IAEA's nuclear security program into the organization's regular budget. In this way, the program would benefit from a larger and more predicable resource base than what its current voluntary character allows for. This action should not preclude additional voluntary contributions (as with the technical cooperation program in the regular budget) that states may choose to make. This recommendation intends to ensure that the IAEA's nuclear security program receives funding to a level commensurate with the large amount of nuclear material requiring protection worldwide.

– Redouble diplomatic efforts to bring into force the amended Convention on the Physical Protection of Nuclear Material, which requires states to enhance the security of nuclear material in domestic use as well as in international transit.

U.S. LEADERSHIP

The Task Force underscores that post–Cold War changes in the security environment call for renewed American leadership to shape U.S. nuclear weapons policy and posture. Many competing interests will demand President Obama's attention. However, urgent nuclear policy issues include the impending expiration of START, the nuclear posture review, and the preparation for the 2010 NPT Review Conference. President Obama has shown an early commitment to this issue with his historic pronouncements in Europe in April 2009 and his call for U.S. leadership on nuclear arms reduction and nonproliferation efforts. The Task Force recommends that the president, the National Security Council, the departments of State, Defense, and Energy, the National Nuclear Security Administration, and the intelligence community should treat the forthcoming nuclear posture review as a thoughtful and serious expression of U.S. nuclear policy, not merely as a bureaucratic exercise, and that the review should give appropriate weight to nonproliferation, nuclear terrorism prevention, arms control, and the credibility of the U.S. deterrent.

The president's involvement with nuclear weapons policy should not stop when the review is completed. He and his senior advisers should receive periodic detailed briefings (annually, unless there is an unusual event requiring more frequent updates) about nuclear weapons posture and targeting, as well as the status of national and international efforts to reduce and secure nuclear weapons-usable materials. In the review and follow-on assessments, the Task Force calls on the administration to determine where the United States can exert even more leadership by reducing, via unilateral action, the amounts of nuclear weapons and fissile material deemed excess to defense needs.

It is too early to know how President Obama's recent groundbreaking declarations will play out, but it is the Task Force's sincere hope that U.S leadership on this issue will lend credibility to U.S. and global efforts to prevent the use of nuclear weapons, curb proliferation, and reduce the threats posed by nuclear weapons and materials.

Additional or Dissenting Views

The key points that I found compelling in the Task Force deliberations are: (1) the United States will need to maintain a credible nuclear deterrent for the foreseeable future; (2) the nuclear stockpiles—deployed warheads, retired weapons awaiting dismantlement, and strategic nuclear material—of the United States, Russia, and other countries, can and should be reduced; (3) it is in the interest of the United States for these stockpile reductions to take place in a transparent manner; (4) the United States must engage Russia and China on nuclear issues if progress is to be made on reducing stockpiles and slowing proliferation—for example, by Iran and North Korea; (5) preventing or reversing a country's move toward the bomb is best achieved by addressing the country's security concerns; coercive international agreements are secondary; (6) the U.S. Department of Energy must adopt a comprehensive plan to support the facilities and people of its nuclear security enterprise that is responsible for weapons R&D, materials production, naval nuclear reactors, associated defense nuclear waste management, and counterproliferation activities.

John Deutch

While I support the many useful recommendations included in this report, it fails in what I believed was to have been its primary goal: to provide a clear and actionable statement of the purposes served by nuclear weapons. A consensus view of this Task Force could have been, I believe, a significant contribution to the current global debate on nuclear weapons policy, and I am disappointed that this opportunity was missed.

Laura S.H. Holgate

This report underscores the importance of a strong nuclear deterrent at the core of a comprehensive strategy that includes valuable steps such as continuing START, securing nuclear weapons and fissile material, exploring missile defense, and transforming cooperative threat reduction programs. Every proposal in the report, however, runs a serious risk that it will not work out as intended. One is reminded of the 1991 Korean Denuclearization Agreement, with its ban on enrichment and reprocessing and additional inspection measures that offered an "NPT-plus" regime, which is still sought for troubled regions. Eighteen years and four administrations later, the United States has instead exposed its inability to enforce compliance even with basic NPT obligations.

In a world of rapid political and technical change, governments are having difficulty making realistic risk assessments, to say nothing of finding workable solutions to complex political and technological dilemmas. Failure on Iran and North Korea now will have great implications for the future. Other issues may be secondary but remain important. For example, START follow-on would benefit from a reexamination of how START I and II addressed stability and verification. Qualitative arms control, such as that in the CTBT and what would be included in a formal antisatellite ban, are likely to have significant unintended consequences as dual-use technology advances.

This report leaves several fundamental questions unanswered. Should the nuclear posture review not allow for flexibility in the types of warheads to be retired, if such flexibility could save money or improve safety and security? Additionally, though the downsides of moving the U.S. weapons complex to the Department of Defense are clear, what should be done to address current dysfunctions?

Ronald F. Lehman II

The disclaimer at the beginning of this report, and the language acknowledging differences among Task Force members in important places within the report, makes it unnecessary for me to dissent. I would like briefly to argue, however, that the discussion of the purposes of U.S. nuclear weapons does not persuasively make the case for their role beyond deterring threats to national survival, nor does it make the case for the need to develop new nuclear weapons, an option that the report does not exclude. Today, only nuclear weapons, and only nuclear weapons of a quantity and quality wielded by states, pose such threats. Other threats discussed in the report—conventional military forces, chemical and potential biological weapons, terrorism, and blackmail—are not of a scale or nature to justify U.S. retention of a deployed nuclear arsenal. To assume otherwise is to miss an opportunity for the United States to lead others in trying to create the conditions necessary to strengthen the international nonproliferation regime and develop robust verification and enforcement practices that could, in decades hence, enable the elimination of all nuclear arsenals.

As long as others possess nuclear weapons or threaten to acquire them, the United States will retain an effective nuclear deterrent. But this report allows for the unhelpful and unnecessary perception that the United States should be more concerned about perpetuating its nuclear arsenal than it is about creating the conditions that would allow all states to live free from the terrifying threat of nuclear war.

George R. Perkovich

I endorse the general policy thrust of this report with one exception. The report states that the current U.S. nuclear doctrine of calculated ambiguity—or threatening to use nuclear weapons in response to a chemical or biological attack—continues to serve U.S. interests. I do not believe that to be the case today. In his April 5, 2009, speech in Prague, President Barack Obama promised that "to put an end to Cold War thinking, [the United States] will reduce the role of nuclear weapons in [its] national security strategy and urge others to do the same." The best way to reduce the role of nuclear weapons in U.S. national security strategy would be to state clearly that the purpose of U.S. nuclear weapons is to deter the use of other states' nuclear weapons against the United States, its allies, and its troops overseas. The current policy of calculated ambiguity is also inconsistent with U.S. negative security pledges given to nonnuclear weapon states at NPT review conferences. Further, it encourages other nuclear weapon states to adopt similar doctrines, rather than encouraging them to reduce the roles that nuclear weapons play in their national security policy.

Scott D. Sagan

This report covers a number of subjects in depth and presents many constructive recommendations. However, it leaves open the possibility of new warhead development. While I support a variety of means for maintaining the existing nuclear stockpile, I strongly feel that these should not include complete replacement or "new" weapons. It is my opinion that the report implies the possible necessity of new warhead designs, a specific point on which I must dissent.

Benn Tannenbaum

Endnotes

1. Some documents subdivide the stockpile into active and inactive elements. The active stockpile is fully functional, including warheads containing tritium, and includes all operationally deployed warheads. Inactive warheads are not fully functional, normally because the tritium has been removed. These categories are important for logistical purposes but are not useful for the Task Force's analysis and are not used in this report.

2. The White House, "The Agenda, Foreign Policy," http://www.whitehouse.gov/agenda/foreign_policy.

3. Barack Obama, "Remarks by President Barack Obama" (speech, Hradcany Square, Prague, Czech Republic, April 5, 2009), http://www.whitehouse.gov/the_press_office/Remarks-by-President-Barack-Obama-in-Prague-as-Delivered.

4. For views on a strategy toward Iran, see *Iran: Time for a New Approach*, Independent Task Force Report No. 52 (New York: Council on Foreign Relations Press, 2004), chaired by Zbigniew Brzezinski and Robert M. Gates. In 2009, CFR also launched an Independent Task Force on Korea.

5. "Remarks by President Barack Obama," April 5, 2009.

6. FAS Strategic Security Blog, "United States Reaches Moscow Treaty Warhead Limit Early," February 9, 2009, http://www.fas.org/blog/ssp/2009/02/sort.php.

7. The White House, "The Agenda, Foreign Policy."

8. "Remarks by President Barack Obama," April 5, 2009.

9. All quotes from the Bush administration's nuclear posture review are from "Nuclear Posture Review [Excerpts]," January 2002, http://www.globalsecurity.org/wmd/library/policy/dod/npr.htm.

10. UK Ministry of Defence, *The Future of the United Kingdom's Nuclear Deterrent*, CM 6994 (London: The Stationary Office, December 2006).

11. See, for example, Robert W. Nelson, "Low-Yield Earth-Penetrating Nuclear Weapons," *Science & Global Security* vol. 10, no. 1 (2002), pp. 1–20.

12. Lewis A. Dunn, Gregory Giles, Jeffrey Larsen, and Thomas Skypek, *Foreign Perspectives on U.S. Nuclear Policy and Posture: Insights, Issues and Implications* (Fort Belvoir, VA: Defense Threat Reduction Agency, 2006).

13. Deepti Choubey, *Are New Nuclear Bargains Attainable?* Carnegie Endowment Report (Washington, DC: Carnegie Endowment for International Peace, October 2008).

14. The Bush administration never sought to develop low-yield nuclear weapons, though the perception that it did is widespread both in the United States and abroad.

15. Major General Polly A. Peyer, chair, *Air Force Blue Ribbon Review of Nuclear Weapons Policies and Procedures* (Washington, DC: Headquarters U.S. Air Force, 2008).

16. North Atlantic Treaty Organization, "NATO's Nuclear Forces in the New Security Environment" (fact sheet, July 1, 2008), http://www.nato.int/issues/nuclear/sec-environment.html.

17. Senate Committee on Foreign Relations, *Convention on Chemical Weapons* (Treaty Doc. 103-21), prepared statement by William J. Perry, 104th Cong., 2d sess., March 28, 1996, p. 123.

18. Charles Aldinger, "U.S. Rules Out Nuclear Attack on Libya Plant," *Washington Post,* May 8, 1996, p. A32. For further analysis of this issue see, for example, Scott Sagan, "The Commitment Trap: Why the United States Should Not Use Nuclear Threats to Deter Biological and Chemical Weapon Attacks," *International Security* vol. 24, no 4 (Spring 2000), pp. 85–115.

19. George P. Shultz, William J. Perry, Henry A. Kissinger, and Sam Nunn, "A World Free of Nuclear Weapons," *Wall Street Journal,* January 4, 2007; Harold Brown and John Deutch, "The Nuclear Disarmament Fantasy," *Wall Street Journal,* November 19, 2007; George P. Shultz, William J. Perry, Henry A. Kissinger, and Sam Nunn, "Toward a Nuclear-Free World," *Wall Street Journal,* January 15, 2008.

20. Anthony Lake, "Confronting Backlash States," *Foreign Affairs,* March/April 1994.

21. John McCain, "An Enduring Peace Built on Freedom: Securing America's Future," *Foreign Affairs,* November/December 2007.

22. "Russia Failing to Meet Nuclear Disarmament Obligations, U.S. State Department Official Says," *Global Security Newswire,* April 14, 2006, http://www.nti.org/d_ newswire/issues/2006/4/14/b732f777-d2e3-4a83-b837-5d0050306f0e.html.

23. Selig Harrison, a U.S. expert on North Korea, said North Korean officials told him that Pyongyang had converted sixty-eight pounds of plutonium into weapons form. See Blaine Harden, "N. Korea Discordant on Obama Era, Nuclear Arsenal," *Washington Post,* January 18, 2009; Korean Central News Agency, "DPRK to Scrap All Points Agreed with S. Korea over Political and Military Issues" (press release, January 30, 2009).

24. U.S. National Intelligence Council, "Iran: Nuclear Intentions and Capabilities," *National Intelligence Estimate,* November 2007 (italics in the original), http://www.dni. gov/press_releases/20071203_release.pdf.

25. Board of Governors, "Implementation of the NPT Safeguards Agreement and Relevant Provisions of Security Council Resolutions 1737 (2006), 1747 (2007), 1803 (2008), and 1835 (2008) in the Islamic Republic of Iran" (report, International Atomic Energy Agency, November 19, 2008), http://www.isis-online.org/publications/iran/iaea-iranreport-111908.pdf.

26. Board of Governors, "Implementation of the NPT Safeguards Agreement and Relevant Provisions of Security Council Resolutions 1737 (2006), 1747 (2007), 1803 (2008), and 1835 (2008) in the Islamic Republic of Iran" (report, International Atomic Energy Agency, February 19, 2009), http://www.isis-online.org/publications/iran/IAEA_ Iran_Report_19Feb2009.pdf.

27. For a more detailed analysis of this issue, see Michael A. Levi, *Deterring State Sponsorship of Nuclear Terrorism,* Council Special Report No. 39 (New York: Council on Foreign Relations Press, 2008).

28. See, for example, David Sanger, "Pakistan, Nuclear Nightmare," *New York Times Magazine,* January 8, 2009.

29. Helene Cooper and Nicholas Kulish, "Biden Signals U.S. Is Open to Russia Missile Deal," *New York Times,* February 8, 2009.

30. Joseph R. Biden Jr., "Remarks by Vice President Biden at the 45th Munich Conference on Security Policy," (speech, Munich, Germany, February 7, 2009), http://www. whitehouse.gov/the_press_office/RemarksbyVicePresidentBidenat45thMunich ConferenceonSecurityPolicy.

31. "Russia May Deploy New-Generation Ballistic Missiles by 2017," RIA Novosti, December 14, 2007.

32. In a November 27, 2007, meeting of the Nuclear Strategy Forum, retired senior Russian military officers stated that the Russian nonstrategic arsenal included 3,800 warheads, of which 1,200 were air defense weapons.

33. Defense Science Board Permanent Task Force on Nuclear Weapons Surety, U.S. Department of Defense, "Report on the Unauthorized Movement of Nuclear Weapons" (Washington, DC, February 2008), http://www.fas.org/nuke/guide/usa/doctrine/usaf/Minot_DSB-0208.pdf.

34. In the U.S.-Russia context, many experts have specifically advised the two sides to refrain from placing multiple warheads on silo-based ICBMs. The destabilizing feature is that one weapon targeted on a single silo could destroy multiple warheads, thus creating a use-or-lose situation in a crisis. Under START II, which never came into force, both sides would have been required to arm ICBMs only with single warheads. Both countries regard START II as dead, although it influenced U.S. force planning through the retirement of the MX/Peacekeeper ICBM and partial de-MIRVing of the Minuteman III force, and may have influenced Russian planning as well. The majority of U.S. ICBMs carry only one warhead.

35. "Remarks by President Barack Obama," April 5, 2009.

36. George N. Lewis and Theodore A. Postol, "European Missile Defense: The Technological Basis of Russian Concerns," *Arms Control Today* vol. 37, no. 8 (October 2007), pp. 13–18.

37. For more details of this program, see http://www.usec.com/megatonstomegawatts.htm.

38. Phil Sewell, "Another Approach to Reducing Access to Weapons-Grade Nuclear Stockpiles" (paper presented to the Tenth Annual International Nuclear Materials Policy Forum, December 15, 2004).

39. Laura S. H. Holgate, "Accelerating the Blend-down of Russian Highly Enriched Uranium" (paper presented at the annual meeting of the Institute for Nuclear Materials Management, July 2005); Michael Knapik, "NTI Study Presents Clearer Picture of Russian HEU Downblending," *NuclearFuel*, August 29, 2005, p. 11.

40. Henry Sokolski, "The Next Arms Race" (draft paper, Nonproliferation Policy Education Center, November 11, 2008).

41. Robert S. Norris and Hans M. Kristensen, "Chinese Nuclear Forces 2008," *Nuclear Notebook* vol. 64, no. 3 (July/August 2008), p. 42; citing Office of the Secretary of Defense, *Annual Report on the Military Power of the People's Republic of China 2008* (Washington, DC: U.S. Department of Defense, 2008), p. 56.

42. Michael D. Maples, Director of the Defense Intelligence Agency, "Annual Threat Assessment, Statement before the Committee on Armed Services, United States Senate," 111th Cong., 1st sess., March 10, 2009, http://armed-services.senate.gov/statemnt/2009/March/Maples%2003-10-09.pdf.

43. Jeffrey Lewis, *The Minimum Means of Reprisal: China's Search for Security in the Nuclear Age* (Cambridge, MA: MIT Press, 2007); Norris and Kristensen, "Chinese Nuclear Forces 2008."

44. Office of the Secretary of Defense, *Annual Report*, p. 24.

45. Robert M. Gates, "A Balanced Strategy: Reprogramming the Pentagon for a New Age," *Foreign Affairs*, January/February 2009.

46. Dennis C. Blair, Director of National Intelligence, "Annual Threat Assessment of the Intelligence Community for the Senate Armed Services Committee," 111th Cong., 1st sess., March 10, 2009, http://intelligence.senate.gov/090212/blair.pdf.

47. People's Republic of China, "China's National Defense in 2006" (Beijing: Information Office of the State Council, December 29, 2006), http://www.fas.org/nuke/guide/china/doctrine/wp2006.html.

48. Bruce W. MacDonald, *China, Space Weapons, and U.S. Security*, Council Special Report No. 38 (New York: Council on Foreign Relations Press, 2008).

49. The dividing line between low-enriched and highly enriched uranium is a 20 percent concentration of the fissile isotope uranium-235. As enrichment increases above this level, the more weapons-usable the enriched uranium becomes. Weapons-grade uranium typically has an enrichment of 90 percent or greater of uranium-235.

50. Gary Samore, ed., *Iran's Strategic Weapons Programmes: A Net Assessment* (London: Routledge, September 2005).

51. The Additional Protocol was formed in response to the safeguards crisis of the 1980s and early 1990s involving Iraq's nuclear program. After the 1991 Gulf War, UN inspectors discovered that Iraq was perhaps within months of developing nuclear weapons despite the fact that comprehensive safeguards had been applied to Iraq's declared nuclear program. The problem was that the "comprehensive" safeguards agreement did not require Iraq to let inspectors into its undeclared facilities, which happened in many cases to be next to declared facilities. Nonetheless, the IAEA had statutory authority to request a special inspection of the undeclared facilities, but the IAEA board of governors had been reluctant for political reasons to allow inspectors to make such inspections.

52. For a related view, see Thomas Shea, "Financing IAEA Verification of the NPT" (paper presented at the NPEC/FRS Conference, November 12–13, 2006).

53. Annex 2 states must meet the criteria of having been a member of the Conference on Disarmament on June 18, 1996, and of being on the IAEA lists of states with nuclear power reactors or research reactors. Using these criteria, Annex 2 includes all of the non-NPT states as well as all states with breakout capability to make nuclear weapons.

54. Robert M. Gates, "Nuclear Weapons and Deterrence in the 21st Century" (speech delivered at the Carnegie Endowment for International Peace, October 28, 2008), http://www.carnegieendowment.org/files/1028_transcrip_gates_checked.pdf.

55. The National Academies, "Academy Addresses Technical Issues in Nuclear Test Ban Treaty" (press release, July 31, 2003); full report, "Technical Issues Related to the Comprehensive Nuclear Test Ban Treaty," http://www.nap.edu/catalog.php?record_id=10471#toc.

56. The Preparatory Commission notes that the planned studies will "highlight progress made in seismology, hydroacoustics, infrasound, and radionuclides monitoring." CTBTO Preparatory Commission, "Want to Join a Global Scientific Project? International Scientific Studies to Evaluate the CTBT Verification Regime," April 2008, http://www.ctbto.org/fileadmin/content/reference/outreach/100408_issleaflet_web.pdf.

57. Safeguard A: conduct a Science Based Stockpile Stewardship program to ensure a safe, secure, and reliable nuclear arsenal; Safeguard B: maintain modern nuclear laboratory facilities and programs; Safeguard C: maintain the capability to resume nuclear test activities; Safeguard D: improve treaty monitoring via a comprehensive research and development program; Safeguard E: assess through a vigorous intelligence program the status of nuclear weapons programs worldwide; and Safeguard F: understand that the president, in consultation with Congress, would be prepared to withdraw from the treaty if the secretaries of defense and energy inform the president that they could no longer certify a high level of confidence in the safety or reliability of a nuclear weapon type deemed critical to the U.S. deterrent force.

58. See, for example, Henry Sokolski and Patrick Clawson, eds., *Getting Ready for a Nuclear Iran* (Carlisle, PA: Strategic Studies Institute, 2005).

59. Michael D. Maples, Director of the Defense Intelligence Agency, "Annual Threat Assessment," Statement before Committee on Armed Services, United States Senate, March 10, 2009.

60. David Albright and Kimberly Kramer, "Civil HEU Watch: Tracking Inventories of Civil Highly Enriched Uranium," in *Global Stocks of Nuclear Explosive Materials* (International Institute for Science and International Security, February 2005), http://www.isis-online.org/global_stocks/end2003/civil_heu_watch2005.pdf.

61. National Nuclear Security Administration, "Global Threat Reduction Initiative: Strategic Plan" (Washington, DC: U.S. Department of Energy, January 2009).

62. See, for example, Anatoli C. Diakov, Alexander M. Dmitriev, Jungmin Kang, Alexey M. Shuvayev, and Frank N. von Hippel, "Feasibility of Converting Russian Icebreaker Reactors from HEU to LEU Fuel," *Science and Global Security* vol. 14 (2006), pp. 33–48.

63. Committee on Medical Isotope Production Without Highly Enriched Uranium, National Research Council, *Medical Isotope Production Without Highly Enriched Uranium* (Washington, DC: National Academy of Sciences Press, 2009).

64. Nuclear Energy Agency, *Nuclear Energy Outlook 2008*, NEA No. 6348 (Paris: OECD Publishing, 2008).

65. For a detailed discussion of these fuel cycle proposals, see, for example, U.S. Committee and Russian Committee on the Internationalization of the Civilian Nuclear Fuel Cycle, National Academy of Sciences and Russian Academy of Sciences, *Internationalization of the Nuclear Fuel Cycle: Goals, Strategies, and Challenges* (Washington, DC: The National Academies Press, 2009).

66. James E. Goodby, "Internationalizing the Nuclear Fuel Cycle," *Bulletin of the Atomic Scientists*, September 4, 2008, http://www.thebulletin.org/web-edition/op-eds/internationalizing-the-nuclear-fuel-cycle.

67. Matthew Bunn, Bob van der Zwaan, John P. Holdren, and Steve Fetter, *The Economics of Reprocessing vs. Direct Disposal of Spent Fuel* (Cambridge, MA: Report for Project on Managing the Atom, Belfer Center for Science and International Affairs, Harvard Kennedy School, December 2003).

68. Charles D. Ferguson, *Preventing Catastrophic Nuclear Terrorism*, Council Special Report No. 11 (New York: Council on Foreign Relations Press, 2006).

69. Levi, *Deterring State Sponsorship of Nuclear Terrorism*.

70. For details, see *Nuclear Forensics: Role, State of the Art, and Program Needs,* joint working group of the American Physical Society and the American Association for the Advancement of Science, 2008.

71. Nuclear Threat Initiative, "NTI in Action: World Institute for Nuclear Security," http://www.nti.org/b_aboutnti/b7_wins.html.

72. DSB Permanent Task Force on Nuclear Weapons Surety, "Report on the Unauthorized Movement of Nuclear Weapons" (Washington, DC: Defense Science Board, February 2008), p. 7, http://www.acq.osd.mil/dsb/reports/2008-04-Nuclear_Weapons_Surety.pdf.

73. Ibid, p. 9.

74. Secretary of Defense Task Force on Nuclear Weapons Management, "Phase I: The Air Force Nuclear Mission," September 2008, p. 2.

75. Peyer, *U.S. Air Force Blue Ribbon Review.*

76. The W89, B90, and W91 were canceled in 1991 and 1992. Kevin O'Neill, "Building the Bomb," chapter one in Stephen I. Schwartz, ed., *Atomic Audit: The Costs and Consequences of U.S. Nuclear Weapons Since 1940* (Washington, DC: Brookings Institution Press, 1998), p. 91.

77. Robert M. Gates and Samuel W. Bodman, "National Security and Nuclear Weapons in the 21st Century" (Washington, DC: U.S. Department of Defense and Department of Energy, November 2008), p. 16, www.defenselink.mil/news/nuclearweaponspolicy.pdf.

78. Robert S. Norris and Hans M. Kristensen, "U.S. Nuclear Forces, 2008," *Bulletin of the Atomic Scientists* vol. 64, no. 1 (March/April 2008), p. 52.

79. "National Security and Nuclear Weapons in the 21st Century," p. 17.

80. Norris and Kristensen, "U.S. Nuclear Forces, 2008," p. 52.

81. The Secretary of Energy Advisory Board report of July 13, 2005, recommended conducting dismantlement at the Nevada Test Site. The Task Force did not evaluate this option, which NNSA in the past has judged infeasible.

82. For much of the Cold War, weapons design was as much an art as a science. Even at the end of the period of nuclear testing, it was primarily an empirical science with significant fundamental issues not fully understood from first principles. Donald MacKenzie and Graham Spinardi, "Tacit Knowledge, Weapons Design, and the Uninvention of Nuclear Weapons," *American Journal of Sociology* vol. 101 (July 1995), pp. 44–99.

83. One concern was that the properties of plutonium would alter due to radioactive decay caused by aging. This concern has been largely eliminated by recent government-sponsored analysis that indicates plutonium aging will not alter nuclear properties until the plutonium is at least eighty-five to one hundred years old, depending on the specific warhead design. NNSA Public Affairs, "Studies Show Plutonium Degradation in U.S. Nuclear Weapons Will Not Affect Reliability Soon" (press release, November 29, 2006), http://nnsa.energy.gov/news/999.htm. Aging of the other components may influence nuclear performance.

84. The W-76 warhead for the Trident submarine was of particular concern because it comprised a large fraction of the day-to-day deployed arsenal, did not have a backup in the event of technical failure, and had been designed to have narrow performance margins because of Cold War concerns with maximizing yield-to-size and weight ratios and minimizing the amount of plutonium used. Weapons scientists suggested taking advantage of the increased weight made available by the reduction in the number of warheads carried on each Trident missile to design a W-76 replacement that would have greater performance margins and thus be less sensitive to aging.

85. NNSA Public Affairs, "NNSA Announces Decisions to Transform National Security Enterprise" (press release, December 16, 2008). NNSA specified the components of the Complex Transformation as: consolidate high-security special nuclear material to five NNSA sites and at fewer locations within these sites, consolidate plutonium operations at NNSA's Los Alamos National Laboratory in New Mexico, consolidate uranium operations at NNSA's Y-12 National Security Complex in Tennessee, keep assembly and disassembly of nuclear weapons and high explosives production and manufacturing at NNSA's Pantex Plant in Texas, consolidate tritium operations at the Savannah River Site in South Carolina, continue flight-testing operations at Tonopah Test Range in Nevada in a more limited scope that relies on a reduced footprint for NNSA operations, and consolidate major environmental test facilities where weapon components are exposed to different temperatures and mechanical stresses, at Sandia National Laboratories in New Mexico.

86. Gates and Bodman, "Nuclear Weapons and Deterrence in the 21st Century."

Task Force Members

Task Force members are asked to join a consensus signifying that they endorse "the general policy thrust and judgments reached by the group, though not necessarily every finding and recommendation." They participate in the Task Force in their individual, not institutional, capacities.

Spencer P. Boyer is the director of international law and diplomacy in the National Security and International Policy Department of the Center for American Progress. He was previously the executive director and War Powers Initiative director at the Constitution Project, based at Georgetown University's Public Policy Institute. Boyer began his professional career as an associate in the international law firm of Jones, Day, Reavis & Pogue and has served with international courts and tribunals in The Hague, Zurich, and Paris. Boyer is a coeditor and contributor to *Power and Superpower: Global Leadership and Exceptionalism in the 21st Century*. He is a graduate of Wesleyan University and received his MA and JD degrees from New York University.

Linton F. Brooks served from July 2002 to January 2007 as administrator of the U.S. Department of Energy's National Nuclear Security Administration, where he was responsible for the U.S. nuclear weapons program and for the department's international nuclear nonproliferation programs. His extensive government experience includes service as the assistant director of the U.S. Arms Control and Disarmament Agency, chief U.S. negotiator for the Strategic Arms Reduction Treaty (where he held the rank of ambassador), director of arms control for the National Security Council, and a number of Navy and U.S. Department of Defense assignments. He is now an independent consultant on national security issues, a senior adviser at the Center for Strategic and International Studies, and a distinguished research fellow at the National Defense University.

Ashton B. Carter* was recently confirmed as undersecretary of defense for acquisition, technology, and logistics. He is on leave from the Harvard Kennedy School, where he was the Ford Foundation professor of science and international affairs and codirector of the Preventive Defense Project. From 1993 to 1996, Carter served as assistant secretary of defense for international security policy. He was twice awarded the Defense Distinguished Service Medal, the highest award given by the Pentagon. For his contributions to intelligence, he was awarded the Defense Intelligence Medal. Before his government service, Carter was the director of the Center for Science and International Affairs at the Harvard Kennedy School. He received bachelor's degrees in physics and medieval history from Yale University and a doctorate in theoretical physics from Oxford University, where he was a Rhodes scholar.

John Deutch is institute professor at the Massachusetts Institute of Technology, where he previously was provost, dean of science, and chairman of the Department of Chemistry. His government career has included serving as director of central intelligence, deputy secretary of defense, and undersecretary of defense (acquisition and technology) in the first Clinton administration, and undersecretary and director of energy research in the U.S. Department of Energy in the Carter administration. He served on the President's Intelligence Advisory Board for President George H.W. Bush and on the President's Science and Technology Advisory Committee for presidents Reagan and Clinton. Deutch is on the boards of Cheniere Energy, Citigroup, and Raytheon. He is a trustee of Resources for the Future, the Center for American Progress, the Urban Institute (life), and the Museum of Fine Arts, Boston.

Charles D. Ferguson is the Philip D. Reed senior fellow for science and technology at the Council on Foreign Relations. He is also an adjunct professor in the security studies program at Georgetown University and an adjunct lecturer in the national security studies program at the Johns Hopkins University. Before arriving at CFR in 2004, he worked as a scientist-in-residence in the Washington, DC, office of the Monterey Institute's Center for Nonproliferation Studies. Ferguson has served as

---

*Carter participated in the Task Force under his affiliation with Harvard University. As a current administration official, he has not been asked to join the Task Force consensus.

a foreign affairs officer in the Bureau of Nonproliferation, U.S. Department of State, where he helped develop policies on nuclear safety and security issues. He has also worked on nuclear proliferation and arms control issues as a senior research analyst and director of the nuclear policy project at the Federation of American Scientists. After graduating with distinction from the U.S. Naval Academy, he served as an officer on a ballistic missile submarine during the Cold War. He holds a PhD in physics from Boston University.

Michèle A. Flournoy* was recently confirmed as undersecretary of defense for policy. Before accepting this post, she was president of the Center for a New American Security (CNAS). Before cofounding CNAS, she was a senior adviser at the Center for Strategic and International Studies and a distinguished research professor at the Institute for National Strategic Studies at the National Defense University. Before that, she was dual-hatted as principal deputy assistant secretary of defense for strategy and threat reduction and deputy assistant secretary of defense for strategy. Flournoy was awarded the Secretary of Defense Medal for Outstanding Public Service in 1996, the Department of Defense Medal for Distinguished Public Service in 1998, and the Chairman of the Joint Chiefs of Staff's Joint Distinguished Civilian Service Award in 2000.

John A. Gordon served in the White House as the president's homeland security adviser from June 2003 until June 2004 and as the deputy national security adviser for counterterrorism and the national director for counterterrorism from June 2002 to June 2003. Before joining the White House team, Gordon was the first administrator of the National Nuclear Security Administration and undersecretary of energy, responsible for the entirety of the nation's nuclear weapons program, serving from June 2000 until June 2002. As an Air Force four-star general, he was the deputy director of central intelligence from October 1997 until June 2000. Gordon's thirty-two-year Air Force career included significant concentration on research and development, strategic planning, missile and space operations, intergovernmental operations, and international negotiations.

---

*Flournoy participated in the Task Force under her affiliation with the Center for a New American Security. As a current administration official, she has not been asked to join the Task Force consensus.

Lisa E. Gordon-Hagerty is president and chief executive officer of LEG Inc., a consulting firm providing strategic advice and counsel in global energy issues. Gordon-Hagerty served as executive vice president and chief operating officer of USEC Inc., the world's leading supplier of enriched uranium fuel for commercial nuclear power plants. She is a former member of the White House National Security Council staff, where she served as director for combating terrorism, overseeing from 1998 to 2003 the federal government's readiness and response to acts of chemical, biological, and nuclear terrorism. Before joining the White House NSC staff, she served for six years at the Department of Energy, where she held positions overseeing several programs, including emergency management, operational emergency response, and the safety and security of the country's nuclear weapons program. Before that, she was a professional staff member of the Energy and Commerce Committee of the U.S. House of Representatives. Gordon-Hagerty began her professional career as a physicist at the Lawrence Livermore National Laboratory.

Eugene E. Habiger is a distinguished fellow and policy adviser with the University of Georgia's Center for International Trade and Security. In his previous assignment as the commander in chief of the U. S. Strategic Command (STRATCOM), he was responsible for all U.S. Air Force and U.S. Navy strategic nuclear forces supporting the national security strategy of strategic deterrence. Before joining the Center for International Trade and Security, General Habiger was the president and CEO of the San Antonio Water System, where he was responsible for general operations along with the strategic long-range business and water resources planning for the ninth-largest city in the United States. He also worked as the Department of Energy's director of security and emergency operations. As the department's security czar, he was charged by the secretary with changing the security culture at the Energy Department and establishing a program to reenergize and restore confidence in the department's security program.

J. Bryan Hehir is the Parker Gilbert Montgomery professor of the practice of religion and public life at the Harvard Kennedy School. He also serves as the secretary for health and social services in the Archdiocese of Boston. From 1973 to 1992, he served on the staff of the U.S. Conference of Catholic Bishops in Washington addressing issues of foreign policy and domestic policy. He served on the faculties of the George-town School of Foreign Service (1984–92, 2002–2003) and the Harvard Divinity School (1993–2001). From 2002 to 2004, he was president of Catholic Charities USA. His teaching and writing focus on ethics and international relations and the role of religion in politics. He is a Mac-Arthur fellow. His writings include "The Moral Measurement of War," "Military Intervention and National Sovereignty," and "Catholicism and Democracy."

Laura S.H. Holgate has served since 2001 as the vice president for Russia/New Independent States Programs at the Nuclear Threat Initiative (NTI). Before joining NTI, Holgate directed the Department of Energy's Office of Fissile Materials Disposition, where she was responsible, from 1998 to 2001, for consolidating and disposing of excess weapons plutonium and highly enriched uranium in the United States and Russia. From 1995 through 1998, she directed the Cooperative Threat Reduction Program (Nunn-Lugar) of U.S. assistance to Russia and other former Soviet states to eliminate the WMD legacy of the Cold War. She holds an AB from Princeton University and an SM from the Massachusetts Institute of Technology, and she spent two years on the research staff at the Harvard Kennedy School. Holgate serves as president of Women in International Security and is a member of the Council on Foreign Relations and the International Institute for Strategic Studies. She participates in advisory panels for the Pacific Northwest National Laboratory and the Oak Ridge National Laboratory.

Frederick J. Iseman is the chairman and chief executive officer of CI Capital Partners LLC (formerly Caxton-Iseman Capital). He chairs CI Capital Partners' portfolio companies in various industries, including a holding company providing homeland security and intelligence training to the U.S. military. He sits on the University Council of Yale and sponsored the Yale Globalization Center's conference on WMD. He is on the advisory board of the Nuclear Threat Initiative and recently sponsored their second U.S.-Russia nuclear nonproliferation conference at the Russian Academy of Science in Moscow. Iseman also serves on the boards of the International Rescue Committee, the Academy for Educational Development, and several museums and operas in New York and St. Petersburg, Russia. He is a member of the International Council of the Belfer Center for Science and International Affairs at the Harvard Kennedy School. He has been published in the *New York Times*, *Harper's Magazine*, the *New Yorker*, and other publications, and his writing has been anthologized in *The Inquiring Reader*.

Arnold Kanter is a principal and founding member of the Scowcroft Group. He served as undersecretary of state from 1991 to 1993. Before assuming this position, he served on the White House staff from 1989 to 1991 as special assistant to the president, and in a variety of capacities in the State Department from 1977 to 1985. In addition to his government experience, Kanter was a program director at the RAND Corporation, a member of the research staff at the Brookings Institution, and a member of the faculty at Ohio State University and the University of Michigan. Previously a member of the Defense Policy Board, Kanter currently serves on the President's Foreign Intelligence Advisory Board, as an adviser to the intelligence community, and on the Government Advisory Board of Convera Technologies. He also is a member of the Council on Foreign Relations (where he chairs the congressional staff roundtable on national security), the Aspen Strategy Group, and the International Institute of Strategic Studies, and is a director of the Atlantic Council and the Stimson Center.

Ronald F. Lehman II is the director of the Center for Global Security Research at the Lawrence Livermore National Laboratory. He is also chairman of the governing board of the International Science and Technology Center, an intergovernmental organization headquartered in Moscow, Russia. He serves as a member of the Department of Defense Threat Reduction Advisory Committee and the Department of State International Security Advisory Board. After the September 11 attacks, he was detailed to the National Nuclear Security Administration to work on counterterrorism and homeland security issues. In 1995, he was appointed to the five-member President's Advisory Board on Arms Proliferation Policy. He was the director of the Arms Control and Disarmament Agency from 1989 to 1993, and served in the Defense Department as assistant secretary for international security policy, in the State Department as chief negotiator on strategic offensive arms, and in the White House as deputy assistant to the president for national security affairs. He has also served on the National Security Council staff as a senior director, in the Pentagon as deputy assistant secretary, on the professional staff of the Senate Armed Services Committee, and in Vietnam with the U.S. Army.

Jack F. Matlock Jr. is a retired diplomat who has held academic posts since 1991 at Columbia University (1991–96, 2007), the Institute for Advanced Study (1996–2001), Princeton University (2001–2004), and Hamilton College (2006). While in the U.S. Foreign Service, Ambassador Matlock served as ambassador to the Soviet Union and to Czechoslovakia and as special assistant to the president. He is the author of *Reagan and Gorbachev: How the Cold War Ended, Autopsy on an Empire*, and a handbook to *Stalin's Collected Works*.

Franklin C. Miller is an independent consultant and a senior counselor at the Cohen Group. Before that, he served in the White House as a special assistant to President George W. Bush and as senior director for defense policy and arms control on the National Security Council staff. His White House assignment capped a thirty-one-year career in the U.S. government, which included two years at the Department of State and twenty-two years serving under seven secretaries in a series of progressively senior positions in the Department of Defense. His final assignments in the Department of Defense were as acting assistant secretary for international security policy from September 1996 to November 1997, principal deputy assistant secretary for strategy and threat reduction from November 1997 to October 2000, and again as acting assistant secretary from October 2000 until January 2001. He also served as the chair of NATO's nuclear policy committee (the High Level Group) from September 1996 to January 2001 and of NATO's counterproliferation policy committee (the Defense Group on Proliferation) from September 1996 to December 1997. Miller currently serves on the U.S. Strategic Command Advisory Group, the Defense Policy Board, and the Sandia National Laboratory's Nuclear Weapons External Advisory Board, and additionally is a senior adviser for the Center for Strategic and International Studies' International Security Program.

George R. Perkovich is vice president for studies at the Carnegie Endowment for International Peace. He is an expert on nuclear strategy and nonproliferation. He is an expert on nuclear strategy and nonproliferation. He is the author of *India's Nuclear Bomb*, which received the Herbert Feis Award from the American Historical Association for outstanding work by an independent scholar, and the A. K. Coomaraswamy Prize from the Association for Asian Studies as an outstanding book on South Asia. Perkovich is coeditor of *Abolishing Nuclear Weapons: A Debate*, and *Universal Compliance: A Strategy for Nuclear Security*, a blueprint for rethinking the international nuclear nonproliferation regime. He has written extensively on the Iranian nuclear challenge. His 2005 essay in *Foreign Affairs*, "Giving Justice Its Due," explores broader issues of values and norms that affect foreign policymaking, including in the nuclear arena. Perkovich served as a speechwriter and foreign policy adviser to Senator Joseph R. Biden Jr. (D-DE) from 1989 to 1990.

William J. Perry is the Michael and Barbara Berberian professor at Stanford University. He is a senior fellow at the Freeman Spogli Institute for International Studies and serves as codirector of the Preventive Defense Project, a research collaboration of Stanford and Harvard universities. Perry was the nineteenth secretary of defense for the United States, serving from February 1994 to January 1997. He previously served as deputy secretary of defense (1993–94), and as undersecretary of defense for research and engineering (1977–81). He is on the board of directors of LGS Innovations and several emerging high-tech companies and is chairman of Global Technology Partners. His previous business experience includes serving as a laboratory director for General Telephone and Electronics (1954–64); founder and president of ESL Inc. (1964–77); executive vice president of Hambrecht & Quist Inc. (1981–85); and founder and chairman of Technology Strategies & Alliances (1985–93). He is a member of the National Academy of Engineering and a fellow of the American Academy of Arts and Sciences. He has received a number of awards, including the Presidential Medal of Freedom (1997). Perry received a BS and MS from Stanford University and a PhD from Penn State, all in mathematics.

Mitchell B. Reiss is currently diplomat-in-residence at the College of William and Mary, where he has held a number of leadership positions. His government service includes director of policy planning at the State Department (2003–2005), special presidential envoy to the Northern Ireland peace process (2003–2007), special assistant to the national security adviser at the White House, and consultant to the Arms Control and Disarmament Agency, the State Department, the Congressional Research Service, and the Los Alamos National Laboratory. Prior to joining William and Mary, Reiss helped start the Korean Peninsula Energy Development Organization (KEDO), a multinational organization dealing with North Korea. Reiss is the author of *Bridled Ambition: Why Countries Constrain Their Nuclear Capabilities* and *Without the Bomb: The Politics of Nuclear Nonproliferation*, and has authored more than eighty articles on international security and arms control issues.

Lynn Rusten is an independent consultant with more than twenty-five years of experience in national security matters. From 2003 to 2008, she was a senior professional staff member of the Senate Armed Services Committee, handling a wide range of foreign and defense policy issues. Rusten has also held a number of positions in the executive branch, including on the secretary of state's policy planning staff and in the Arms Control and Disarmament Agency, where she was an adviser to the U.S. START delegation. Before joining the executive branch, she was director of the National Academies of Sciences' Committee on International Security and Arms Control. She received a BA in government from Oberlin College, an MA in Russian and East European studies from the University of Michigan, and an MS in national security strategy from the National War College.

Scott D. Sagan is a professor of political science and codirector of Stanford's Center for International Security and Cooperation. Before joining the Stanford faculty, Sagan was a lecturer in the Department of Government at Harvard University and served as a special assistant to the director of the Organization of the Joint Chiefs of Staff in the Pentagon. He has also served as a consultant to the Office of the Secretary of Defense and at the Sandia National Laboratory and the Los Alamos National Laboratory. Sagan is the author of *Moving Targets: Nuclear Strategy and National Security*, *The Limits of Safety: Organizations, Accidents, and Nuclear Weapons*, and, with coauthor Kenneth N. Waltz, *The Spread of Nuclear Weapons: A Debate Renewed*. He is coeditor with Peter R. Lavoy and James L. Wirtz of the book *Planning the Unthinkable*. His latest edited volume, *Inside Nuclear South Asia*, will be released in September 2009.

Brent Scowcroft is the resident trustee of the Forum for International Policy. He served as the national security adviser to both presidents Ford and Bush. Born in Utah, he graduated from West Point and served in the Air Force in a number of capacities, including assistant air attaché in Belgrade, Yugoslavia, special assistant to the director of the Joint Chiefs of Staff, and military assistant to President Nixon. From 1978 to 1987, General Scowcroft remained actively engaged in national security affairs, serving on the President's Advisory Committee on Arms Control, the Commission on Strategic Forces, and the President's Special Review Board, also known as the Tower Board. He earned a doctorate in international relations from Columbia University.

Benn Tannenbaum is associate program director at the Center for Science, Technology, and Security Policy at the American Association for the Advancement of Science (AAAS), focusing on connecting scientists with government on security matters. Before joining AAAS, Tannenbaum was a senior research analyst for the Federation of American Scientists, where he worked extensively on the paper *Flying Blind*. Tannenbaum also served as the 2002–2003 American Physical Society congressional science fellow. During his fellowship, he worked for Representative Edward J. Markey (D-MA) on nonproliferation issues. He has testified before the U.S. House of Representatives Committee on Homeland Security and has authored or coauthored over 160 scientific or policy-related publications. Tannenbaum earned his PhD in experimental particle physics from the University of New Mexico.

Task Force Observers

Observers participate in Task Force discussions, but are not asked to join the consensus. They participate in their individual, not institutional, capacities.

Michael A. Levi is the David M. Rubenstein senior fellow for energy and the environment at the Council on Foreign Relations. His interests center on the intersection of science, technology, and foreign policy. He is director of the CFR program on energy security and climate change and was project director for the CFR-sponsored Independent Task Force on Climate Change. He is the author of the book *On Nuclear Terrorism* and coauthor with Michael O'Hanlon of *The Future of Arms Control*. Levi holds an MA in physics from Princeton University and a PhD in War Studies from King's College London.

Gary Samore* is the White House coordinator for arms control and the prevention of WMD proliferation and terrorism at the National Security Council. Formerly, he was vice president, director of studies, and Maurice R. Greenberg chair at the Council on Foreign Relations. From 2001 to 2005, he was director of studies and senior fellow for non-proliferation at the International Institute for Strategic Studies. Samore served at the National Security Council from 1995 to 2001. He began his career there as the director for nonproliferation and export controls and then became the special assistant to the president and senior director for nonproliferation and export controls. Before his career led him to the National Security Council, Samore spent seventeen years working at the Department of State, where he served as special assistant to the ambassador-at-large for nonproliferation and nuclear energy policy. He later served as the acting director and deputy director at the Office of Regional

*Samore participated as a Task Force observer under his affiliation with the Council on Foreign Relations.

Nonproliferation, Bureau of Political-Military Affairs, and then as the deputy to Ambassador-at-Large Robert Gallucci.

Elizabeth Sherwood-Randall* is special assistant to the president and senior director for European affairs at the National Security Council. Formerly, she was an adjunct senior fellow for alliance relations at the Council on Foreign Relations, a senior research scholar at the Stanford Center for International Security and Cooperation, and a senior adviser to the Preventive Defense Project. Sherwood-Randall served as deputy assistant secretary of defense for Russia, Ukraine, and Eurasia from 1994 to 1996. Previously, she was associate director of the Harvard Strengthening Democratic Institutions Project, chief foreign affairs and defense policy adviser to Senator Joseph R. Biden Jr., and a guest scholar at the Brookings Institution. She received her bachelor's degree from Harvard College and doctorate in International Relations at Oxford University, where she was a Rhodes scholar.

Francis Slakey holds an endowed position at Georgetown University, where he is the Cooper/Upjohn professor of science and public policy and the codirector of the program on science in the public interest. He has written widely on science policy issues, publishing more than fifty articles for the popular press, including the *New York Times, Washington Post,* and *Scientific American.* He is a fellow of the American Physical Society, a MacArthur scholar, and currently a Lemelson research associate of the Smithsonian Institution. Slakey is the associate director of public affairs for the American Physical Society.

---

*Sherwood-Randall participated as a Task Force observer under her affiliation with the Council on Foreign Relations.

Independent Task Force Reports

Published by the Council on Foreign Relations

Confronting Climate Change: A Strategy for U.S. Foreign Policy
George E. Pataki and Thomas J. Vilsack, Chairs; Michael A. Levi, Project Director
Independent Task Force Report No. 61 (2008)

U.S.-Latin America Relations: A New Direction for a New Reality
Charlene Barshefsky and James T. Hill, Chairs; Shannon O'Neil, Project Director
Independent Task Force Report No. 60 (2008)

U.S.-China Relations: An Affirmative Agenda, A Responsible Course
Carla A. Hills and Dennis C. Blair, Chairs; Frank Sampson Jannuzi, Project Director
Independent Task Force Report No. 59 (2007)

National Security Consequences of U.S. Oil Dependency
John Deutch and James R. Schlesinger, Chairs; David G. Victor, Project Director
Independent Task Force Report No. 58 (2006)

Russia's Wrong Direction: What the United States Can and Should Do
John Edwards and Jack Kemp, Chairs; Stephen Sestanovich, Project Director
Independent Task Force Report No. 57 (2006)

More than Humanitarianism: A Strategic U.S. Approach Toward Africa
Anthony Lake and Christine Todd Whitman, Chairs; Princeton N. Lyman and J. Stephen Morrison, Project Directors
Independent Task Force Report No. 56 (2006)

In the Wake of War: Improving Post-Conflict Capabilities
Samuel R. Berger and Brent Scowcroft, Chairs; William L. Nash, Project Director; Mona K. Sutphen, Deputy Director
Independent Task Force Report No. 55 (2005)

In Support of Arab Democracy: Why and How
Madeleine K. Albright and Vin Weber, Chairs; Steven A. Cook, Project Director
Independent Task Force Report No. 54 (2005)

Building a North American Community
John P. Manley, Pedro Aspe, and William F. Weld, Chairs; Thomas d'Aquino, Andrés Rozental, and Robert Pastor, Vice Chairs; Chappell H. Lawson, Project Director
Independent Task Force Report No. 53 (2005)

Iran: Time for a New Approach
Zbigniew Brzezinski and Robert M. Gates, Chairs; Suzanne Maloney, Project Director
Independent Task Force Report No. 52 (2004)

An Update on the Global Campaign Against Terrorist Financing
Maurice R. Greenberg, Chair; William F. Wechsler and Lee S. Wolosky, Project Directors
Independent Task Force Report No. 40B (Web-only release, 2004)

Renewing the Atlantic Partnership
Henry A. Kissinger and Lawrence H. Summers, Chairs; Charles A. Kupchan, Project Director
Independent Task Force Report No. 51 (2004)

Iraq: One Year After
Thomas R. Pickering and James R. Schlesinger, Chairs; Eric P. Schwartz, Project Consultant
Independent Task Force Report No. 43C (Web-only release, 2004)

Nonlethal Weapons and Capabilities
Paul X. Kelley and Graham Allison, Chairs; Richard L. Garwin, Project Director
Independent Task Force Report No. 50 (2004)

New Priorities in South Asia: U.S. Policy Toward India, Pakistan, and Afghanistan
(Chairmen's Report)
Marshall Bouton, Nicholas Platt, and Frank G. Wisner, Chairs; Dennis Kux and Mahnaz
Ispahani, Project Directors
Independent Task Force Report No. 49 (2003)
Cosponsored with the Asia Society

Finding America's Voice: A Strategy for Reinvigorating U.S. Public Diplomacy
Peter G. Peterson, Chair; Kathy Bloomgarden, Henry Grunwald, David E. Morey, and
Shibley Telhami, Working Committee Chairs; Jennifer Sieg, Project Director; Sharon
Herbstman, Project Coordinator
Independent Task Force Report No. 48 (2003)

Emergency Responders: Drastically Underfunded, Dangerously Unprepared
Warren B. Rudman, Chair; Richard A. Clarke, Senior Adviser; Jamie F. Metzl, Project
Director
Independent Task Force Report No. 47 (2003)

Iraq: The Day After (Chairs' Update)
Thomas R. Pickering and James R. Schlesinger, Chairs; Eric P. Schwartz, Project Director
Independent Task Force Report No. 43B (Web-only release, 2003)

Burma: Time for Change
Mathea Falco, Chair
Independent Task Force Report No. 46 (2003)

Afghanistan: Are We Losing the Peace?
Marshall Bouton, Nicholas Platt, and Frank G. Wisner, Chairs; Dennis Kux and Mahnaz
Ispahani, Project Directors
Chairman's Report of an Independent Task Force (2003)
Cosponsored with the Asia Society

Meeting the North Korean Nuclear Challenge
Morton I. Abramowitz and James T. Laney, Chairs; Eric Heginbotham, Project Director
Independent Task Force Report No. 45 (2003)

Chinese Military Power
Harold Brown, Chair; Joseph W. Prueher, Vice Chair; Adam Segal, Project Director
Independent Task Force Report No. 44 (2003)

Iraq: The Day After
Thomas R. Pickering and James R. Schlesinger, Chairs; Eric P. Schwartz, Project Director
Independent Task Force Report No. 43 (2003)

Threats to Democracy: Prevention and Response
Madeleine K. Albright and Bronislaw Geremek, Chairs; Morton H. Halperin, Director;
Elizabeth Frawley Bagley, Associate Director
Independent Task Force Report No. 42 (2002)

America—Still Unprepared, Still in Danger
Gary Hart and Warren B. Rudman, Chairs; Stephen E. Flynn, Project Director
Independent Task Force Report No. 41 (2002)

Terrorist Financing
Maurice R. Greenberg, Chair; William F. Wechsler and Lee S. Wolosky, Project Directors
Independent Task Force Report No. 40 (2002)

Enhancing U.S. Leadership at the United Nations
David Dreier and Lee H. Hamilton, Chairs; Lee Feinstein and Adrian Karatnycky, Project
Directors
Independent Task Force Report No. 39 (2002)
Cosponsored with Freedom House

Improving the U.S. Public Diplomacy Campaign in the War Against Terrorism
Carla A. Hills and Richard C. Holbrooke, Chairs; Charles G. Boyd, Project Director
Independent Task Force Report No. 38 (Web-only release, 2001)

Building Support for More Open Trade
Kenneth M. Duberstein and Robert E. Rubin, Chairs; Timothy F. Geithner, Project
Director; Daniel R. Lucich, Deputy Project Director
Independent Task Force Report No. 37 (2001)

Beginning the Journey: China, the United States, and the WTO
Robert D. Hormats, Chair; Elizabeth Economy and Kevin Nealer, Project Directors
Independent Task Force Report No. 36 (2001)

Strategic Energy Policy Update
Edward L. Morse, Chair; Amy Myers Jaffe, Project Director
Independent Task Force Report No. 33B (2001)
Cosponsored with the James A. Baker III Institute for Public Policy of Rice University

Testing North Korea: The Next Stage in U.S. and ROK Policy
Morton I. Abramowitz and James T. Laney, Chairs; Robert A. Manning, Project Director
Independent Task Force Report No. 35 (2001)

The United States and Southeast Asia: A Policy Agenda for the New Administration
J. Robert Kerrey, Chair; Robert A. Manning, Project Director
Independent Task Force Report No. 34 (2001)

Strategic Energy Policy: Challenges for the 21st Century
Edward L. Morse, Chair; Amy Myers Jaffe, Project Director
Independent Task Force Report No. 33 (2001)
Cosponsored with the James A. Baker III Institute for Public Policy of Rice University

A Letter to the President and a Memorandum on U.S Policy Toward Brazil
Stephen Robert, Chair; Kenneth Maxwell, Project Director
Independent Task Force Report No. 32 (2001)

State Department Reform
Frank C. Carlucci, Chair; Ian J. Brzezinski, Project Coordinator
Independent Task Force Report No. 31 (2001)
Cosponsored with the Center for Strategic and International Studies

U.S.-Cuban Relations in the 21st Century: A Follow-on Report
Bernard W. Aronson and William D. Rogers, Chairs; Julia Sweig and Walter Mead, Project Directors
Independent Task Force Report No. 30 (2000)

Toward Greater Peace and Security in Colombia: Forging a Constructive U.S. Policy
Bob Graham and Brent Scowcroft, Chairs; Michael Shifter, Project Director
Independent Task Force Report No. 29 (2000)
Cosponsored with the Inter-American Dialogue

Future Directions for U.S. Economic Policy Toward Japan
Laura D'Andrea Tyson, Chair; M. Diana Helweg Newton, Project Director
Independent Task Force Report No. 28 (2000)

First Steps Toward a Constructive U.S. Policy in Colombia
Bob Graham and Brent Scowcroft, Chairs; Michael Shifter, Project Director
Interim Report (2000)
Cosponsored with the Inter-American Dialogue

Promoting Sustainable Economies in the Balkans
Steven Rattner, Chair; Michael B.G. Froman, Project Director
Independent Task Force Report No. 27 (2000)

Non-Lethal Technologies: Progress and Prospects
Richard L. Garwin, Chair; W. Montague Winfield, Project Director
Independent Task Force Report No. 26 (1999)

Safeguarding Prosperity in a Global Financial System: The Future International Financial Architecture
Carla A. Hills and Peter G. Peterson, Chairs; Morris Goldstein, Project Director
Independent Task Force Report No. 25 (1999)
Cosponsored with the International Institute for Economics

U.S. Policy Toward North Korea: Next Steps
Morton I. Abramowitz and James T. Laney, Chairs; Michael J. Green, Project Director
Independent Task Force Report No. 24 (1999)

Reconstructing the Balkans
Morton I. Abramowitz and Albert Fishlow, Chairs; Charles A. Kupchan, Project Director
Independent Task Force Report No. 23 (Web-only release, 1999)

Strengthening Palestinian Public Institutions
Michel Rocard, Chair; Henry Siegman, Project Director; Yezid Sayigh and Khalil Shikaki, Principal Authors
Independent Task Force Report No. 22 (1999)

U.S. Policy Toward Northeastern Europe
Zbigniew Brzezinski, Chair; F. Stephen Larrabee, Project Director
Independent Task Force Report No. 21 (1999)

The Future of Transatlantic Relations
Robert D. Blackwill, Chair and Project Director
Independent Task Force Report No. 20 (1999)

U.S.-Cuban Relations in the 21st Century
Bernard W. Aronson and William D. Rogers, Chairs; Walter Russell Mead, Project Director
Independent Task Force Report No. 19 (1999)

After the Tests: U.S. Policy Toward India and Pakistan
Richard N. Haass and Morton H. Halperin, Chairs
Independent Task Force Report No. 18 (1998)
Cosponsored with the Brookings Institution

Managing Change on the Korean Peninsula
Morton I. Abramowitz and James T. Laney, Chairs; Michael J. Green, Project Director
Independent Task Force Report No. 17 (1998)

Promoting U.S. Economic Relations with Africa
Peggy Dulany and Frank Savage, Chairs; Salih Booker, Project Director
Independent Task Force Report No. 16 (1998)

U.S. Middle East Policy and the Peace Process
Henry Siegman, Project Coordinator
Independent Task Force Report No. 15 (1997)

Differentiated Containment: U.S. Policy Toward Iran and Iraq
Zbigniew Brzezinski and Brent Scowcroft, Chairs; Richard W. Murphy, Project Director
Independent Task Force Report No. 14 (1997)

Success or Sellout? The U.S.-North Korean Nuclear Accord
Kyung Won Kim and Nicholas Platt, Chairs; Richard N. Haass, Project Director
Independent Task Force Report No. 2 (1995)
Cosponsored with the Seoul Forum for International Affairs

Nuclear Proliferation: Confronting the New Challenges
Stephen J. Hadley, Chair; Mitchell B. Reiss, Project Director
Independent Task Force Report No. 1 (1995)

To purchase a printed copy, call the Brookings Institution Press: 800.537.5487.
Note: Task Force reports are available for download from CFR's website, www.cfr.org.
For more information, email publications@cfr.org.